D0075875

DOMESTIC MARIJUANA

Recent Titles in
Contributions in Criminology and Penology

Doing Time in American Prisons: A Study of Modern Novels
Dennis Massey

Demographics and Criminality: The Characteristics of Crime in America
Ronald Barri Flowers

Taking Charge: Crisis Intervention in Criminal Justice
Anne T. Romano

Beyond Punishment: A New View on the Rehabilitation of Criminal Offenders
Edgardo Rotman

Police Pursuit Driving: Controlling Responses to Emergency Situations
Geoffrey P. Alpert and Roger G. Dunham

Vigilantism: Political History of Private Power in America
William C. Culberson

Chinese Subculture and Criminality: Non-traditional Crime Groups in America
Ko-lin Chin

A Sword for the Convicted: Representing Indigent Defendants on Appeal
David T. Wasserman

Delinquency in Puerto Rico: The 1970 Birth Cohort Study
Dora Nevares, Marvin E. Wolfgang, and Paul E. Tracy with the Collaboration of Steven Aurand

Waging the Battle Against Drunk Driving: Issues, Countermeasures, and Effectiveness
Gerald D. Robin

Policing Western Europe: Politics, Professionalism, and Public Order, 1850-1940
Clive Emsley and Barbara Weinberger, editors

Policing a Socialist Society: The German Democratic Republic
Nancy Travis Wolfe

DOMESTIC MARIJUANA

A NEGLECTED INDUSTRY

Ralph A. Weisheit

Contributions in Criminology and Penology, Number 35
James Inciardi, Series Adviser

GREENWOOD PRESS
New York • Westport, Connecticut • London

Library of Congress Cataloging-in-Publication Data

Weisheit, Ralph A.
    Domestic marijuana : a neglected industry / Ralph A. Weisheit.
      p. cm.—(Contributions in criminology and penology, ISSN
0732-4464 ; no. 35)
    Includes bibliographical references and index.
    ISBN 0-313-28040-1 (alk. paper)
    1. Marihuana industry—United States. I. Title. II. Series.
HD9019.M382U68 1992
338.1'7379'0973—dc20   91-34695

British Library Cataloguing in Publication Data is available.

Library of Congress Catalog Card Number: 91-34695
ISBN: 0-313-28040-1
ISSN: 0732-4464

First published in 1992

Greenwood Press, 88 Post Road West, Westport, CT 06881
An imprint of Greenwood Publishing Group, Inc.

Printed in the United States of America

The paper used in this book complies with the
Permanent Paper Standard issued by the National
Information Standards Organization (Z39.48-1984).

10 9 8 7 6 5 4 3 2 1

Copyright Acknowledgments

The author and publisher gratefully acknowledge the following:

Sage Publications, Inc., for excerpts from Weisheit, R. A. (1991). The
intangible rewards from crime. The case of domestic marijuana cultivation.
Crime and Delinquency. 37(4): 506-527. © 1991. Reprinted by permission of
Sage Publications, Inc.

Federal Legal Publications, Inc., for excerpts from Weisheit, R. A. (1991).
Drug use among marijuana growers. *Contemporary Drug Problems*. (18)2:
191-217.

For Carol and Ryan

CONTENTS

ILLUSTRATIONS   ix

ACKNOWLEDGMENTS   xi

1   A Neglected Industry   1

2   A Brief History of Marijuana   11

3   Marijuana and the Law   21

4   The Rise of the Domestic Marijuana Industry   31

5   Marijuana Botany and Cultivation   53

6   The Research Setting   61

7   Who Grows and Why   71

8   Issues Related to Growing   101

9   A Law-Enforcement Perspective   135

10   Policy Implications   155

APPENDIX A: RESEARCH DESIGN AND PLAN   159

APPENDIX B: FEDERAL MARIJUANA LAWS   169

BIBLIOGRAPHY   175

INDEX   183

ILLUSTRATIONS

FIGURES

4.1   Fifteen States with the Most Cultivated Marijuana
        Eradications in 1990   37

6.1   Cultivated Marijuana Plots Eradicated by County, 1987–1989   66

6.2   Wild Marijuana Plots Eradicated by County, 1987–1989   67

TABLES

4.1   Estimated Domestic Marijuana Production, 1982–1989 in
        Metric Tons   33

4.2   Value of Marijuana and Other Cash Crops for 1988–1989   35

4.3   1990 Domestic Cannabis Eradication/Suppression Program,
        Cultivated Plants Eradicated   36

6.1   Correlation Between Marijuana Eradication in Illinois
        Counties in 1987–1989 and Selected Social and
        Economic Factors   69

ACKNOWLEDGMENTS

In the earliest stages of this research I received helpful feedback from Jim Inciardi and important financial support from Illinois State University. As my thinking about the issue developed, I sought outside support and was eventually funded by a grant from the National Institute of Justice (NIJ Grant #88-IJ-CX-0016). The opinions expressed here are those of the author and do not necessarily represent those of the National Institute of Justice. I would like to thank Bernard Gropper from NIJ, who was particularly patient with a new grantee.

I was fortunate to have two very competent and conscientious staff members assisting me throughout the project: Kathleen Patrecia Mott and Anna Wells. While it would be impossible to list everything they did, a partial listing reflects their importance to the project. Ms. Mott was primarily responsible for making telephone contacts with officials, transcribing tapes, fielding telephone inquiries, assembling materials, scheduling interviews, and mailing. Ms. Wells focused on identifying cases, locating and analyzing secondary data sources, and scheduling interviews. She was instrumental in making sense of the federal and state statutes regarding marijuana and wrote the first draft of the summary of those statutes in chapter 3. Both Ms. Wells and Ms. Mott also provided valuable feedback on the final project report.

I would also like to thank the many growers, officials, and nameless others who agreed to be interviewed and provided feedback. These people had little to gain personally. On a topic as sensitive as drugs, where each side has a good reason to be suspicious of "outsiders" asking questions, I appreciated their candor and trust.

Finally, I would like to thank my wife, Carol, for her support, my son, Ryan, for helping me keep my work in perspective, and my parents, Lenus and Sarah Weisheit, for their longstanding support and encouragement.

DOMESTIC MARIJUANA

1

A NEGLECTED INDUSTRY

Domestic marijuana cultivation was not officially recognized as a problem until 1982. In that year the government was able to check the amount of domestic marijuana seized against its first official estimate of domestic production. As it turned out, 38 percent more domestic marijuana was *seized* in 1982 than was even thought to *exist* (Warner, 1986). Since most authorities estimate that seizures represent only 10 to 20 percent of the marijuana available, the size of the discrepancy was astounding. The failure of officials to come even close to estimating the domestic marijuana crop on their first try reflected the extent to which marijuana growing was largely an invisible enterprise.

By the late 1980s the estimated size of the domestic industry continued to expand. It was thought that between 1 and 2 million people were growing marijuana recreationally, and as many as 250,000 were growing it commercially. The federal government estimated that between 1985 and 1988 the amount of marijuana produced in the United States doubled to nearly 5,000 metric tons (National Narcotics Intelligence Consumers Committee, 1989). If marijuana cultivation was considered an industry, its annual revenues easily approached $60 billion (see chapter 4). The impact of domestic marijuana production on the domestic marijuana market has been substantial. Between one-fourth and one-half of the marijuana consumed in the United States is produced in this country, and as early as 1982 U.S. marijuana was thought to constitute as much as 10 percent of the marijuana used in Canada (Stamler, Fahlman & Vigeant, 1985).

By the late 1980s marijuana was routinely found growing in every state in the union, and law enforcement was becoming more sophisticated and determined in its efforts to eradicate domestic crops. By 1987, 48 states were taking part in the Drug Enforcement Administration's Domestic Marijuana Eradication Program. Further, more local and state police were trained to detect plants and record seizures with more precision, not only counting seized plants but also categorizing them on the basis of potency and the cultivation technique used.

Many of the elements that set the stage for an expanding domestic marijuana industry are explored in this book, but three factors have been vital to this expansion: First, the hemp plant, also known as marijuana (sometimes spelled *marihuana*), is relatively easy to grow, and flourishes in a variety of climates. Because marijuana came primarily from Mexico and Southeast Asia in the 1960s, people mistakenly assumed that the plant required a tropical climate to thrive. In fact, the plant can adapt to a wide variety of climates, including those of the northernmost parts of the United States. In 1990, for example, the northern state of Michigan ranked seventh in the seizure of cultivated marijuana plants, Minnesota ranked eleventh, and Wisconsin ranked fifteenth (Drug Enforcement Administration, 1990). All of these states seized more cultivated marijuana than such arid states as Texas, New Mexico, or Arizona. Second, since the 1960s the selling price of marijuana has skyrocketed. While an ounce of marijuana could be purchased for as little as $30 in the 1960s, by 1991 it was common for high potency marijuana to sell quite literally for its weight in gold, and there were scattered reports of marijuana selling on the street for three times its weight in gold. Finally, the demand for marijuana is so strong that cultivators seldom have problems finding buyers. On the contrary, interviews conducted during the course of this study suggested chronic shortages of high-potency marijuana.

Given these facts regarding the ease of growing marijuana and the profits to be made, the interesting question is not why marijuana growing has become more common but why so little is known about it—why it remains an invisible industry. The primary function of this book is to describe commercial marijuana cultivation in the United States. Before doing that, however, it will be helpful to consider why such a large industry has been given so little attention.

WHY HAS THE INDUSTRY BEEN NEGLECTED?

Given its size and the increased attention of law enforcement, it may seem surprising that the domestic marijuana industry has received so little attention. During the course of this study three factors emerged that would account for this oversight: (1) the rural setting in which marijuana growing takes place, (2) the nature of the marijuana industry, and (3) marijuana's place in the war on drugs.

Rural Setting

Overlooking marijuana cultivation in rural areas cannot be explained solely as a result of the absence of drugs in these communities. Not only are drugs part of rural communities, but rural areas are increasingly used to produce synthetic drugs and the rate of marijuana use has rapidly approached that of urban areas. Rural areas are also essential in the movement of imported drugs (e.g., heroin, cocaine) across the country. Rural Kentucky, for example, is not only a major producer of marijuana, but it has also been an important transshipment point for cocaine (Potter & Gaines, 1990). And, just as drug producing countries eventually develop problems with drug consumption (Inciardi, 1986), rural transshipment points are also likely to develop problems with drug consumption. During the course of this study, for example, some marijuana growers in Kentucky were reportedly using the profits from their operations to support cocaine habits.

Similarly, while a number of researchers have emphasized the role of poverty and urban decay as factors in urban drug trafficking, it has been all but ignored in rural areas. Poverty is not just an urban phenomenon, however. Weinberg (1987) has noted that "only 6 of 159 high-poverty counties in 1979 contained a city of 25,000 population (401)."

The rural setting in which most large marijuana fields are found presents challenges regarding both geography and culture. In terms of geography, the media, special police drug units, and researchers are more often centered in urban areas and focus on drug issues in the urban environment. To urban observers of the drug scene, the domestic marijuana industry has been largely invisible.

The wide geographic dispersion of marijuana producers continues to limit research and media attention on the issue and was a major obstacle for law enforcement until the mid-1980s. Before then, marijuana detection and eradication were almost exclusively a local responsibility, usually headed by rural county sheriffs, who are among the most underfunded and understaffed of law enforcement agencies. During the 1980s, however, the federal government became more involved in eliminating domestic marijuana. For example, the 1989 *National Drug Control Strategy* listed specific federal objectives for marijuana eradication, including a doubling of federal funding between FY 1989 and FY 1990 (Office of National Drug Control Policy, 1989). At the same time, there have been increased cooperative efforts across jurisdictions, such as the formation of task forces that include county sheriffs and the state police. Despite the increased attention on rural drug enforcement, there are still comparatively more drug arrests in urban areas. Castellano and Uchida (1990) estimate the rate of drug arrests in urban areas to be nearly four times that in rural counties. They also argue that because most drug enforcement is proactive, variations in arrest rates among jurisdictions are more the result of differences in enforcement efforts than of differences in consumption patterns.

For researchers, the fact that marijuana cultivation cases are widely dispersed has meant that studying the problem is very labor-intensive. In this study, for example, it was common for a single interview to require from two to three hours of travel each way. By comparison, the logistics of interviewing drug dealers and users in a single neighborhood or section of a city are simple. Researchers in rural environments also have a smaller base of published research studies from which to work. While there are hundreds of books on urban studies, there are relatively few on rural life and culture in the United States, as a visit to any research library will show.

For the national media, the issue is not only physical distance but is also an urban bias that is partly a result of where television and radio stations are located, partly a result of the urban backgrounds of news personnel, and partly a result of "playing" to such large markets as New York, Chicago, and Los Angeles by taking urban problems and portraying them as national (Epstein, 1973). This bias emerged in the 1980s when the national media portrayed crack cocaine as a problem that had permeated "main street U.S.A.," when in reality there was little evidence that it was widespread outside a few large urban areas. Stories about marijuana cultivation are rural curiosities, which are thought to be primarily of local interest.

Aside from geography, studies of drugs in rural areas must contend with rural culture. In particular, rural communities are often closed to outsiders, and rural citizens may be reluctant to tell outsiders about local deviants. An example of the self-imposed isolationism of rural areas is given in Kessler's description of the problems in establishing a legal services program in a rural community:

> The norms of cooperation, trust and courtesy shared by members of the local bar apply exclusively to attorneys with strong local roots. In general, the legal community is unreceptive to lawyers from outside the county using their local court. Further, members of the local legal community are suspicious of, if not openly hostile to, lawyers born and raised outside the county opening a practice within the county. The attitudes of the legal community to outsiders are illustrated in the comments of one veteran local attorney: "If you're part of the community, practicing law here can be great. But it's not particularly pleasant for out-of-county people. There's a very tight knit organization over here that doesn't particularly care for the outsider." (Kessler, 1990:274–75)

For researchers, the subjects of urban drug studies are from areas and cultures with which they already have some familiarity. An urban drug researcher would find it very difficult to penetrate and understand the rural culture in many parts of the United States. The current study provides an illustration. A local sheriff was reluctant to be interviewed about growers in his area, agreeing only after he was told he was recommended by a state trooper with whom he had worked. The sheriff began the interview by vaguely describing a local case and casually throwing out questions to "test" the researcher. For example: "The grower was a sorgum farmer—but being from the city you wouldn't know what that is. Would you?" As it turned out I was from a rural community and knew something of sorgum farming. After I passed his "test" by answering a series of similar questions, the tone of the interview changed to openness and cooperation. The interview lasted for several hours and was very informative. I left with the clear impression that his concern was that a stranger would be insensitive to local feelings and would paint an inaccurate (and unflattering) picture of the community. It was also my impression that a researcher with little knowledge of rural life would not have gotten very far in the interview, finding the sheriff polite but not very talkative.

Finally, many rural areas of the United States operate on cash economies, even for relatively large purchases. Long-time residents who purchase cars and household appliances with cash are not likely to arouse much suspicion (unless their spending becomes excessive by local standards). Similarly, the nature of farming makes the masking of supplemental cash income much simpler than is true for those whose income is derived from fixed salaries or hourly wages.

Of course, not all growers are in remote rural areas and not all rural areas are so closed, but these elements appear with enough frequency to make the thorough study of marijuana growers difficult, particularly for outsiders. They also have the effect of hiding much marijuana growing from public visibility.

The Nature of the Marijuana Industry

The very nature of marijuana growing contributes to its low profile. Upper-level cocaine or heroin dealers and smugglers operate on a relatively short time frame. Deals can be consummated quickly and the dealer may have actual possession of the drug for only a brief time. Quick and large profits are inviting to those prone to conspicuous consumption and short-run hedonism (Adler, 1985; Mills, 1986). By comparison, commercial marijuana growers operate within a longer time frame. During the four to seven months in which growers tend their crops, they are either in continuous possession of the plants or at least make frequent visits to tend the crops. Furthermore, becoming proficient at growing usually takes several tries (i.e., seasons), and even more time may be needed to locate strains that are best suited to the local climate and that produce the desired type of high (see chapter 5). Tied to the land and working with a relatively bulky plant, the commercial grower is best served by *inconspicuous* consumption and a lifestyle that does not draw the attention of others.

Further contributing to the low visibility of marijuana growers is the highly decentralized nature of the industry. Though some very large networks exist, smaller independent operators are more typical. The arrest and prosecution of small independents simply draws less public and police interest than does the break-up of large networks. This low visibility is similar to that of smuggling, where more attention is focused on large operations than on the low-level "mules" who carry drugs across the border.

Marijuana and the War on Drugs

It is ironic that during the drug war of the 1980s, when law enforcement came to recognize marijuana growing as a problem, the momentum for enforcement activity was away from marijuana and toward hard drugs. Arrests related to marijuana declined from 72.4 percent of all drug arrests in 1976 to 33.9 percent in 1988. At the same time, heroin and cocaine arrests rose from 9.9 percent of all drug arrests in 1976 to 52.0 percent in 1988 (Federal Bureau of Investigation, 1977; 1989). Similarly, the media's focus on cocaine, and later crack cocaine, diverted attention away from marijuana.

Marijuana cultivation may also have escaped serious scrutiny because it does not fit neatly into existing images of the drug business. While the public generally supports criminal sanctions for the possession of marijuana, most do not view it in the same sinister terms used to describe heroin or cocaine. The ambiguous feelings toward marijuana can be illustrated by:

- The number of politicians who have admitted to past marijuana use while now advocating harsh penalties for casual or experimental users. These "confessions" seem to have had little impact on the careers of these politicians, while similar admissions about the prior use of heroin or cocaine would have had far more serious implications.

- Although at one time eleven states had decriminalized marijuana, all have reversed their positions, and there is now strong opposition to allowing marijuana for medical uses (e.g., glaucoma and relieving the nausea from cancer treatments). At the same time, the law does allow the medical use of cocaine and such powerfully addictive narcotics as morphine and codeine.

- While the public generally favors strong criminal sanctions for marijuana use, most do not think marijuana use should preclude people from holding positions of trust. For example, the decision to withdraw Douglas Ginzburg's nomination to the Supreme Court because of allegations of marijuana use and perhaps even sales was criticized by a number of people who were otherwise strongly antidrug.

Drawing public attention to marijuana production also raises general questions about drug policies. The public seems most content defining the drug problem as the product of "foreign" influences, particularly those from South America and Southeast Asia. At the same time, there is a reluctance to recognize that the same economic pressures that allow coca farmers to justify their actions also permit low-level drug dealers and manufacturers to justify their activities. In the same way, economic issues can be used to justify continued government subsidies to tobacco farmers, although the government itself recognizes that tobacco is both addicting and harmful. The parallel with tobacco is especially apt. In the major marijuana cultivation state of Kentucky, for example, marijuana growing is most frequent in economically depressed rural counties that can support few legal agricultural crops other than tobacco.

Examples of the larger questions raised by a focus in marijuana cultivation include:

- How can we hold South American governments accountable for coca production over a territory spanning millions of acres of remote forest and mountains when we cannot control the cultivation of marijuana within our own borders? The wealth and resources of the United States certainly far outstrip those of any South American country.

- How can we use ships and planes to put an impenetrable wall around drug-producing countries (as has been suggested) when we cannot stop the flow of marijuana (a relatively bulky drug) from Hawaii, a set of small remote islands that we control? The state of Hawaii is consistently among the top producing states for domestic marijuana.

- If the principle of crop substitution for Colombian coca crops is such an excellent idea, why hasn't it been applied to those rural areas of the United States where marijuana growing is common?

   In short, domestic marijuana cultivation forces us to think of the drug problem as a domestic problem in a way that is simply not true for other drugs. And because the drug is marijuana, a host of contradictory attitudes are brought to the fore. Of course, conflicting sentiments underly all of our drug policies, from alcohol to heroin, but no other drug has such a large gap between the harshness of criminal penalties (see chapter 3) and the level of public tolerance (as evidenced by the large number of users).

CONCLUSIONS

   This book is the product of an ongoing study of U.S. marijuana cultivators, with a particular focus on commercial operations. When I began the study in 1988, I was struck by how little was known about these growers or the industry of which they were a part. The police were in no position to have lengthy and candid discussions with growers. The academic community had virtually ignored them, and journalistic accounts tended to be both superficial and focused on unusual cases.
   The primary data for this study came from interviews with marijuana growers and officials in Illinois. These were supplemented by interviews with officials from other states, including Indiana, Kentucky, Missouri, Tennessee, and Hawaii. In addition, a few interviews were conducted with growers outside of Illinois, as well as with the editors of two magazines about marijuana cultivation (one now defunct), two directors of the National Organization for the Reform of Marijuana Laws, two authors of books about marijuana cultivation, and reporters who had covered cases in other states (see Appendix A for a full discussion of methodological issues). While logistical issues made an emphasis on Illinois a practical choice, the supplemental interviews suggest that the themes identified in this study transcend this single location.
   I was initially drawn to the topic by publicity surrounding the arrest of several farmers in Illinois for commercially growing marijuana. A preliminary look at these growers suggested they were longtime community members in good standing. And because the Midwest is a major source of domestic marijuana, it seemed likely that other farmers might be involved. Two of these cases are illustrated in the following newspaper accounts.

   Case 1: An Illinois farmer was arrested for growing approximately two acres of marijuana on his 300-acre farm. The 40-
   year-old man was a lifelong resident of the community of
   1,300. He was a veteran who "was called upon to deliver
   patriotic addresses on the 4th of July, Armistice Day and
   meetings of the local VFW." Working with the farmer were
   two police officers who had been friends since childhood. The

town was shocked and the mayor was quoted as saying "Next, you'll be telling me they've got the minister and the bank president." (Smith, 1987)

Case 2: A 30-year-old farmer was arrested for growing 1,400 marijuana plants among rows of corn and soybeans. The plants were started indoors in a windowless growing room and then transplanted outdoors in the spring, where they were watered through an elaborate irrigation system. He had apparently been growing marijuana for several years and may have used banks in the Bahamas to launder the drug money. He pled guilty but requested that he be released prior to sentencing because "I'm a farmer, your honor, I have crops in the field to get out." ("Knox Farmer Pleads Guilty," 1987; Williams, 1987)

From newspaper accounts and other public sources, it was not clear whether these farmers were themselves drug users, but it appeared they had no history of criminal arrests—drug-related or otherwise. Both the people and the setting stood in stark contrast to most studies of the urban drug trade. Further, these farmers did not fit existing descriptions of marijuana growers in northern California (see, for example, Chapple, 1984; Raphael, 1985).

The study is not limited to legitimate farmers but includes marijuana growers from a wide range of backgrounds. Nevertheless, it was shaped by questions about how farmers became involved in marijuana growing, particularly older farmers with little evidence of prior experience in the drug business. Public accounts of these cases, combined with journalistic accounts from other parts of the country (primarily California and Kentucky) were used to generate a typology of growers, described in chapter 4. The typology was used as a reference point throughout the study and guided the research, which in turn, led to modifications of the typology.

The study was driven by four overlapping objectives: First, to develop basic information about a poorly understood phenomenon, domestic marijuana growing; this effort included learning about characteristics of growers, the conditions under which growing emerges and persists, and the process by which some people exit the business. Second, to assess and modify the typology of growers developed from public accounts of these cases. Third, to gauge community reaction to a marijuana arrest, since in a rural setting there may be a strong response to publicly identifying one of its members as a marijuana grower. This objective has implications for both the likelihood that an arrested grower will return to growing and the general deterrent effect of making these arrests public in rural areas. Finally, to consider whether some of the techniques successfully used in urban drug studies could be applied in rural areas, since almost nothing is known about the methodological issues involved in conducting research of this type and in these settings. Thus, the study was designed to address both broad substantive questions about growing and more focused questions of method.

I approached the problem with an open mind and a determination to be a neutral observer whose role was to provide an accurate portrayal of growers. While the study might have led me to adopt a firm ideological stance—whether pro- or anti-marijuana—that did not happen. Instead I have come away with a heightened appreciation of the complexity of the issue and a continuing fascination with both growers and the police who try to find them.

The book is laid out to place the study of marijuana growers in an historical and national context, while still recognizing features that may make growers in Illinois unique from those in other parts of the country. Chapter 2 provides a brief history of marijuana, including the legal cultivation of the hemp plant during World War II, a legacy of particular relevance to midwestern states. Chapter 3 outlines the legal context in which marijuana cultivation occurs, including the use of forfeiture in these cases. Chapter 4 summarizes what is known about the nature and distribution of marijuana cases throughout the United States and how the nature and extent of production is thought to have changed in recent years. Chapter 5 describes the botany of marijuana, the nature of which places constraints on marijuana production, poses challenges to growers, and is used by officials trying to locate plots. Chapter 6 details the geography and culture in which Illinois marijuana cultivation occurs, including social factors and their relationship to patterns of growing. Chapter 7 uses interviews with growers to describe their characteristics and to explore issues related to the experience of growing. Chapter 8 continues to utilize interview data to describe the arrest and its impact on the grower, including the response of the community. Chapter 9 examines many of the issues raised by growers but does so by using the perspectives of law enforcement officers familiar with marijuana cultivation cases. This chapter also uses interviews with people familiar with marijuana growing outside of Illinois, to suggest common themes and regional variations in its cultivation. Finally, chapter 10 outlines several policy implications raised by this study.

The findings presented here are intended not only to be interesting in their own right, but also to encourage others to examine this fascinating and important topic.

2

A BRIEF HISTORY
OF MARIJUANA

While domestic cultivation has only recently been discovered as a problem for law enforcement, marijuana itself has a long history, both in the United States and throughout the world. Contemporary patterns emphasize the use of marijuana as an intoxicant, but historically intoxication was only one of many uses for the plant. Thus, to understand contemporary marijuana production it is useful to understand the social history of marijuana and derived products. Like any mind altering drug, the effects of marijuana and society's reaction to it cannot be understood by considering only its chemical action on the body. It is equally important to understand the social and cultural context in which the drug is used (Zinberg, 1984).

ORIGINS OF MARIJUANA

The precise origins of marijuana are unknown, but it is believed that the plant originated in western China or central Asia (Merlin, 1972). Marijuana has been cultivated throughout recorded history and probably dates from much earlier. The plant produces not only a drug but a strong fiber that has long been used in the manufacture of fine linen, paper, canvas, and rope. The first paper and the first cloth were probably made from hemp fibers. Until 1883, between 75 and 90 percent of all paper in the world was made from hemp fiber, including the paper used to print the Gutenberg Bible and the first two drafts of the Declaration of Independence (Herer, 1990).

Compared with cotton, hemp is softer, warmer, more water absorbent and has three times the tensile strength (Herer, 1990). Until the 1900s, hemp was used for nearly all ships' sails, "rigging, anchor ropes, cargo nets, fishermen's nets, flags, shrouds, and oakum (the main sealant for ships against salt water for use between loose or green beams)" (Herer, 1990:5). The oil of the plant resembles linseed oil and is valuable because paints made with it dry quickly. Oil from marijuana seeds had long been used to make soap and for illumination, and the residues created by the extraction of oil were used as fishbait and fertilizer (Reininger, 1966). In addition, the seeds have been used as birdseed, and the leaves, flowering tops, and resin have been used for a variety of religious and medical purposes.

Although hemp played an important role in early America and now grows wild in many U.S. states, it did not originate in this country. It came here through a circuitous route that involved industrial, medicinal, and recreational uses for the plant. The focus now shifts to briefly tracing the historical path that brought marijuana to the United States.

ASIA AND EUROPE

Marijuana can be traced to at least 10,000 B.C. on the island of Taiwan, off the coast of China, and the oldest preserved specimen of hemp dates to the Chou dynasty (1122–256 B.C.), where it was used in cloth (Abel, 1976;1980). The Chinese are also credited with the invention of paper, which was probably first made from hemp. The Chinese not only knew the utility of hemp for making fabric and paper but recognized its medicinal and intoxicating properties as well. One of the earliest references to marijuana is in a Chinese document dated from 2737 B.C. in which marijuana was described as a medicine (Merlin, 1972). Emperor Shen-Nung, who lived during the twenty-eighth century B.C. and came to be recognized as the father of Chinese medicine, wrote about cannabis in what was to become a standard manual on drugs in China (Abel, 1976). He recommended hemp "for everything from rheumatism to absent-mindedness" (Frazier, 1974:13). The Chinese also mixed cannabis with alcohol to produce a painkiller used in medical procedures.

Marijuana also has a long history of use as an intoxicant and medicine in India, dating at least several thousand years before Christ. Written documents refer to it in India as early as 2000 B.C. and in the Middle East as early as 650 B.C. Abel (1980) has described India as the first marijuana-oriented culture and notes that marijuana came to have important religious significance. At the end of the nineteenth century the Indian Hemp Commission was formed to examine the use of cannabis in India and to consider placing restrictions on its availability. The commission concluded that "the plant was so much an integral part of the culture and religion of that country that to curtail its usage would certainly lead to unhappiness, resentment, and suffering" (Abel, 1980:21).

Marijuana was well established in the Islamic world by A.D. 1000, and in later years Arabs spread the use of marijuana to Africa and the Mediterranean and eventually to Europe. A common method for consuming marijuana, particularly in India and the Middle East, was to ingest the resin from female marijuana plants rather than smoking or burning the leaves directly. This resin is also known as hashish.

In the Middle East, the word *hashish* was originally used to describe marijuana. Some argue that the word comes from an Arabic term for grass, fodder, medicinal herbs, or weeds (Abel, 1982). Others suggest that the words *hashish* and *assassin* are both derived from the name Hashishin, a Middle Eastern religious fanatic who lived about A.D. 1100 (Taylor, 1966). In either case, the term *hashish* was originally used to describe marijuana in general and only later came to describe the substance made from the plant's resin.

In contrast to Asia and the Middle East, few Europeans appeared to use marijuana as an intoxicant but depended heavily on the plant for making cloth and rope. While most Americans today think of marijuana as something to be smoked, the practice of smoking marijuana did not begin until the 1500s and 1600s, after the introduction of tobacco to Europe. Before this time marijuana was eaten or added to foods. In some very early societies (e.g., 2500 B.C.) groups of people would not smoke marijuana in a cigarette or pipe but would burn it in a tent or other small enclosure and breathe in the fumes. Still other groups would throw piles of it onto a campfire and stand nearby to inhale the fumes. Frazier (1974) cites evidence that on some parts of the Asian continent, near Mongolia, flowering tops of hemp plants were burned in cone-shaped tents designed to collect the fumes for inhalation.

As an intoxicant, the Greeks and Romans preferred alcohol to marijuana, but they were aware of marijuana and used it extensively for its fiber (Abel, 1976). Some have suggested that the drug written about by Homer was marijuana. There may also be several references to marijuana in the Old Testament of the Bible (Brecher, 1972), although some dispute this contention (Walton, 1938).

AFRICA

Marijuana has a long and extensive history of use in Africa, although it is not native to that continent. It was probably brought by Arab traders many years before Europeans settled there. In Africa marijuana was smoked by most races and for a variety of reasons, including as a painkiller for women during childbirth and during "coffee breaks" for men working in mines. In some parts of Africa hemp cults arose in which hemp was the center of the society and played an important role in religious and social events. In such cults marijuana was not only used for pleasure and recreation but as a punishment (Reininger, 1966). An adulterer, for example, might be required to smoke until he passed out. If further punishment were deemed necessary, "He would then be stripped, pepper would be dropped into his eyes and/or a thin ribbon would be drawn through his nasal bone. More serious crimes were accompanied by additional punishments" (Abel, 1980:145). It has also been suggested that while Europeans used hemp extensively for its fiber, they were unaware of its intoxicating power until they observed African tribesmen eating and smoking hemp leaves (Abel, 1980).

SOUTH AMERICA

It appears that marijuana first entered the United States (as a recreational drug in smokable form) through South America and was introduced to South America from Africa. The word *marijuana* is derived from the Spanish word *maraguango*, referring to any substance producing intoxication. In South America this word was broadly used to describe a variety of intoxicating plants (Walton, 1938) and before that was the term for a poor grade of tobacco (Taylor, 1966).

The first South American country in which marijuana was commonly used was Brazil, where smoking marijuana first became popular in the 1700s. There is almost no doubt that marijuana was brought to Brazil through the slave trade, probably in the 1600s. All of the Brazilian names for marijuana (maconha, macumba, diamba, liamba, pungo, etc.) are African words from the various languages and dialects spoken by the original slaves (Goldman, 1979). It is still true that some of the most potent marijuana grown in this hemisphere comes from Brazil.

From its very beginning in Brazil there were official efforts to limit the use of marijuana. In 1823, for example, when most people in Europe did not know what marijuana intoxication was, Rio de Janeiro passed statutes requiring fines and short jail stays for any slave caught smoking marijuana.

Marijuana soon moved its way up the South American continent to Mexico, where it was commonly used. Soldiers in the Mexican army were reportedly large consumers of marijuana (Bonnie & Whitebread, 1974). It is also said that Pancho Villa's army of peasants was composed largely of people who were stoned most of the time, a condition recalled in the song "La Cucaracha" (Goldman, 1979). In addition, marijuana was commonly administered to fighting animals in Mexico, particularly in the case of cock fighting (Walton, 1938).

Latin American cultures also demonstrate the extent to which the effects of a drug are shaped by the circumstances under which it is taken. In the United States, for example, marijuana smoking is associated with passivity and a reluctance to engage in violence, while in many Latin American countries marijuana is associated with violence, just as alcohol is in this country (Goldman, 1979; Bonnie & Whitebread, 1974).

THE UNITED STATES

It is unclear just how marijuana first came to this country, although it appears that hemp, hashish, and smokable marijuana were discovered at different times and were used in different contexts. Marijuana was probably not used for recreational intoxication in early America but did play an important role in industry and medicine.

Industrial Uses

There is no record that the Pilgrims brought hemp with them, but settlers did bring it to Jamestown in 1611 and cultivated it for its fiber. Its importance for cloth and rope had long been recognized in England, however, and King James I ordered the settlers to produce it for export to England (Grinspoon, 1977). From the early 1600s until after the Civil War, hemp was a major crop in North America and by the 1700s it was important for the economy of many states, with some states even offering rewards for high production and imposing penalties on those who did not produce it (Brecher, 1972). It has been estimated that by 1630 half of winter clothing and nearly all summer clothing of American colonists was made from hemp fibers (Rosevar, 1967).

In 1765 George Washington was growing hemp at Mount Vernon. While he was primarily interested in growing it for fiber, there is also evidence that he was concerned with separating male and female plants before pollination and in increasing the potency of the plant. These activities suggest he also had medical uses in mind for marijuana (Andrews & Vinkenoog, 1967).

By the 1800s the center of hemp production was Kentucky, where roads were built and slaves traded as part of the hemp industry, but the plant was used almost entirely for the manufacture of cloth and rope. Following the Civil War, production declined as cheaper imported hemp was available and as the invention of the cotton gin and cotton and wool machinery made these fabrics cheaper alternatives to hemp for making cloth. (Brecher, 1972).

The Marijuana Tax Act of 1937 effectively banned both the industrial and recreational use of marijuana. This ban was partially lifted from 1942 through 1945, during World War II. During this period, the Japanese cut off U.S. supplies of hemp and other fiber from the Philippines. The United States responded by encouraging U.S. farmers, particularly those in the Midwest, to grow "Hemp for Victory." "The Department of Agriculture provided seeds, fertilizer, machines and planting instructions" (Frazier, 1974:65) to help farmers gear up for production as quickly as possible. In Kentucky and Tennessee hemp was grown for seed stock and hemp for fiber was grown in Wisconsin, Iowa, Illinois, Minnesota, Kentucky, and Indiana. The peak year for production was 1943 when 146,200 acres of hemp were harvested for fiber (U.S.D.A.

Agricultural Statistics, 1944; 1945; 1946). The fibers were used to make a variety of military items. Herer (1990) colorfully illustrates the importance of hemp to the U.S. war effort. He notes that long before he became president, George Bush bailed out of his burning military airplane and was picked up at sea without realizing that (1) hemp seed oil was used to lubricate parts of his aircraft engine, (2) his parachute webbing was made from hemp, (3) hemp was used to make all of the riggings and rope on his rescue ship, (4) firehoses on the ship were made from h:mp, and (5) the stitching in his military boots was of hemp fiber. As the war came to an end so did the industrial applications for hemp in the United States.

Some have suggested that the Marijuana Tax Act of 1937 was motivated in part by economic interests—more specifically, by corporate investments in a new process for making paper from wood pulp rather than hemp (Herer, 1990). It is probably also true that industrial uses for hemp would have assured its continued production had it not been for the development of strong synthetic fibers. As is shown below, however, sentiments against marijuana were fueled by concerns about its recreational use, particularly by minorities and fringe groups, such as jazz musicians and artists. And although it once played an important part in American medicine, by the time of the 1937 Marijuana Tax Act it had only limited acceptance by the medical community. Taken together, these factors tended to overshadow the value of hemp's practical applications.

Medical Uses

Although hemp was used primarily to manufacture cloth and rope, early Americans also recognized the medicinal value of marijuana. Marijuana was first mentioned as a medicine in an American medical text in 1843 and in 1854 was listed as a medicine in the U.S. Dispensatory (Abel, 1980). Cannabis was used, not only for a variety of purely physical ailments, but as a treatment for psychological problems as well. In the 1850s recommended uses for marijuana included the treatment of gout, rheumatism, tetanus, opiate withdrawal symptoms, alcohol withdrawal, loss of appetite, menstrual cramps, convulsions, depression, delirium tremens, insanity, and asthma. In fact, marijuana was officially recognized as a medicine in the *U.S. Pharmacopoeia* and could be prescribed by doctors for a variety of ailments until 1937 when Congress passed the Marijuana Tax Act (Grinspoon, 1977; Himmelstein, 1983).

Although available to physicians as a medicine, marijuana was never widely popular in the medical community. It was used on a limited basis during the Civil War for the treatment of diarrhea and dysentery among soldiers (Abel, 1980). As a drug, marijuana had several limitations. The potency of commercially available marijuana varied greatly and the effects of the drug seemed to vary considerably from patient to patient. In addition, since it was not soluble in water, it could not be given by injection. Further, "the action of cannabis was extremely slow and a doctor might have to remain with his patient for more than an hour after he swallowed the drug to make sure that not only was it having a desired effect, but also that the dosage had not been too high" (Abel, 1980:184). These problems, combined with the fact that some patients had adverse effects from high doses, prevented marijuana from becoming a widely used medicine.

Recreational Uses

While people were well aware of its intoxicating effects, marijuana was not generally used as a recreational drug in the United States until the early 1900s. Even then its use was centered among Mexican laborers who brought it across the border and on certain fringe groups, such as jazz musicians. Much of the pressure for federal legislation regulating marijuana arose, not from the Federal Bureau of Narcotics (FBN) itself, but from local law enforcement in the South and Southwest, who saw it as directly linked to violent crime and to the "problem" of Mexican immigrants (Walton, 1938; Galliher & Walker, 1977). Thus, from early on, the recreational use of marijuana was associated with Mexican workers in Texas and eventually throughout the West and Southwest, and efforts to control the drug often had strong racial overtones (Musto, 1973; Himmelstein, 1983).

Beginning in the late 1920s, there was a growing campaign to educate Americans about the evils of marijuana. It was commonly believed to be a narcotic and to be highly addictive. Even the medical community contributed to these impressions by arguing that while marijuana addiction was different from the experience of addiction to the opiates, in many ways it was more sinister (Bonnie & Whitebread, 1974). Marijuana was blamed for increases in violent crime, sexual promiscuity, and even insanity. Marijuana use came to be synonymous with deviant lifestyles, and several prisons reported that inmates were smuggling in seeds and planting them on prison grounds (Walton, 1938). It was a short step from thinking that "bad people use marijuana" to "marijuana makes people bad." In the 1930s, the chief of detectives of the Los Angeles Police Department was quoted as saying:

> In the past we have had officers of this department shot and killed by marihuana addicts and we have traced the act of murder directly to the influence of marihuana, with no other motive. We have found from long experience and dealing with this type of criminal that marihuana is probably the most dangerous of all our narcotic drugs (quoted in Walton, 1938:32–33).

Race and class prejudices fueled these images, justified the harsh treatment of marijuana users, and facilitated the passage of tough antimarijuana legislation at the local, state, and federal levels. These images of marijuana led it to be defined as a national menace when it was believed that marijuana use was spilling over to the white population (Bonnie & Whitebread, 1974).

In the early 1900s the center for the importation and use of marijuana was New Orleans, where sailors from South America and the West Indies brought the drug with them and Mexican immigrants brought the drug through the Gulf. During World War I, the navy frequently used the port of New Orleans and was concerned about corrupting its sailors on leave. With the help of local authorities the navy closed down the largest red-light district in New Orleans. The jazz musicians who were driven from this area took their music and their marijuana up the Mississippi to Chicago (Himmelstein, 1983; Goldman, 1979).

During the early 1900s, America's favorite drug, alcohol, was on its way to being banned and was already seen by many as evil and harmful. Ironically, prohibiting alcohol may have played a significant role in the "discovery" of marijuana as a recreational drug by Americans. For some, particularly in the jazz world, alcohol was evil but marijuana was actually beneficial. Louis Armstrong, for example, the king of jazz in both New Orleans and Chicago, was a heavy user of marijuana until he died. He believed that alcohol was evil and that marijuana improved his performance (Goldman, 1979). It is fitting then that one of the classic studies of becoming a marijuana user was done by Howard Becker in the 1960s and was based on his experiences playing with a jazz band (Becker, 1963). Until the 1960s, marijuana was seen by the public as an exotic drug used only by artists, musicians, and movie stars—and this perception had a ring of truth to it.

Marijuana was never a widely used recreational drug until the 1960s. For example, the first Gallup Poll on marijuana was done in 1969 and found that 4 percent of the American people had used the drug at least once. By 1977, 24 percent had used it at least once (Brecher, 1972). The widespread use of marijuana was not limited to college students but had been adopted by a broad range of citizens, including as many as 69 percent of soldiers serving in Vietnam (Robins, Helzer, & Davis, 1975).

Studies of high school seniors, college students, and young adults found that between 1975 and 1987 marijuana has shown a steady decline in popularity (Johnston, O'Malley, & Bachman, 1988). To illustrate this trend, the data for high school seniors is discussed below, although the pattern also fits college students and other young adults, for whom shorter time spans are available.

In 1975, 40 percent of high school seniors reported having used marijuana in the prior year. This number rose to 51 percent in 1979 and thereafter declined steadily until 1987, when only 36 percent of seniors reported marijuana use in the prior year. Not only had the *number* of marijuana users declined, but so had the self-reported level of intoxication among users.

Over time, high school seniors also modified their views about marijuana and about the role of the law in regulating marijuana. In the class of 1975, 43 percent thought that regular marijuana use was harmful, and this figure dropped to 35 percent in 1978. By 1987, about three-fourths of high school seniors thought regular use was harmful. In the early surveys seniors generally saw tobacco as more harmful than marijuana but after 1982 marijuana came to be seen as more harmful. Similarly, reported disapproval of regular marijuana users rose from a low of 66 percent in 1977 to 89 percent in 1987.

High school seniors also changed their views regarding marijuana laws. In 1975, 27 percent thought "using marijuana should be entirely legal." Support for legalization rose until 1977 (33 percent), after which it declined to 15 percent in 1987. At no time during this period was legalization the view of the majority.

Overall, the research of Johnston, O'Malley, and Bachman (1988) reflects the declining popularity of marijuana among young people. Despite this, marijuana remains the most popular of the illicit drugs. High school seniors in the class of 1987 were three times more likely to use marijuana than to use stimulants (the next most popular category of illicit drug), and they were three-and-a-half times more likely to use marijuana than cocaine.

SUMMARY

Marijuana has a long history of manufacturing, medical, religious, and recreational applications. The earliest records of marijuana are found in China and other parts of Asia, where it was used in religious ceremonies, as a medicine, and to make paper. From Asia, marijuana was transported through India and into the Middle East. From there it spread to Europe and Africa.

As an industrial product, hemp came to the United States from England. Later, the practice of using marijuana as a recreational drug came from South America and Mexico. Marijuana was outlawed by the federal government with the Marijuana Tax Act of 1937. Despite its illegal status and the possibility of harsh penalties, marijuana became a widely popular recreational drug in the 1960s and 1970s. Marijuana's popularity began to wane in the 1980s, though it remains the most popular of illicit drugs.

3

MARIJUANA AND THE LAW

Much like their feelings toward alcohol, Americans have exhibited ambiguous feelings about the "evils" of marijuana. Some view it as little different from heroin, while others see it as no more harmful than tobacco. These ambiguous views have been reflected in changing social policies toward marijuana. The following discussion gives a brief history of marijuana legislation in the United States and outlines federal and state marijuana laws in effect during the course of this project.

THE DEVELOPMENT OF U.S. LAWS AGAINST MARIJUANA

In the mid-1930s the federal government, under the guidance of Harry Anslinger, led an all-out campaign against marijuana to convince the public that it was a highly dangerous drug and to push for legislation to outlaw it. Numerous stories were told about ax murderers driven to the act by the use of a single marijuana cigarette and women who became prostitutes because of the effects of the drug. In addition, most of the public equated recreational marijuana use with low-status or deviant groups, such as Mexican laborers, jazz musicians, and poor blacks (Musto, 1973).

"Between the mid-30s until the mid-1960s there was a strong public consensus that marijuana was a dangerous drug and that moderate use was impossible" (Himmelstein, 1986:4). All use was considered dangerous and even government hearings on marijuana described the drug as more dangerous than heroin or cocaine (Bonnie & Whitebread, 1974). In many states the criminal penalties for marijuana were identical to those for heroin.

In 1937 the federal government passed the Marijuana Tax Act, which had the effect of criminalizing marijuana possession, and by 1940 every state had outlawed marijuana. In the 1950s state and federal penalties were increased. By 1965 typical marijuana laws included penalties of two years in prison for the first offense of simple possession, five years for the second offense, and ten years for the third offense. Penalties for selling were even harsher, and except for first offenders, people who were convicted of simple possession had mandatory sentences with no opportunity for parole or probation. Some states had unusually harsh penalties by current standards. In Alabama, for example, simple possession carried a mandatory minimum of five years, and in Missouri a second offense for possession could bring a life sentence. In Georgia, a second conviction for sale to minors could be punishable by death (Himmelstein, 1986; Inciardi, 1981). During the 1960s the local police, who had previously ignored minor marijuana violations, responded to community pressure and began emphasizing marijuana arrests (DeFleur, 1975).

All of this began to change in the late 1960s, however. The 1970 Comprehensive Drug Abuse Prevention and Control Act rewrote the federal law and separated marijuana from narcotic drugs. At the federal level both simple possession and nonprofit distribution of small amounts were changed from felonies to misdemeanors (Himmelstein, 1986). In addition, first offenders could have their criminal records expunged. Many states copied these federal efforts, and within a few years all but Nevada had reduced simple possession of marijuana to a misdemeanor (see Galliher & Cross, 1982, for a discussion of marijuana laws in Nevada).

In 1972 the National Commission on Marijuana and Drug Abuse recommended decriminalization or partial prohibition that would keep penalties for selling but remove them for personal use and nonprofit distribution of small amounts. Although some were critical of decriminalization, it drew support from a wide range of groups, both liberal and conservative. The conservative William F. Buckley, Jr., for example, openly supported decriminalization (Himmelstein, 1986).

By 1978 eleven states, with one-third of the American population, had decriminalized marijuana use. Thirty others had provisions for conditional discharge (charges dropped or no penalty attached), and twelve allowed for the expungement of record for first-possession offenders. Even President Jimmy Carter was recommending decriminalization at the federal level (Koski & Eckberg, 1983).

What brought about these changes? First, other federal agencies, including the National Institute on Drug Abuse, that were not primarily law-enforcement-oriented (as the DEA was) were brought into the debate. These agencies made possible the open discussion of differing points of view on the topic.

Second, and most important, marijuana was more and more being used by middle-class youth. Nebraska, for example, became one of the first states to reduce marijuana possession to a misdemeanor in 1969 as the result of a case in which the sons of a prominent county prosecutor and a university professor were charged with possession. Similarly, the son of a U.S. senator spent time in jail for simple possession (Himmelstein, 1986).

The rise of middle- and upper-class users not only put political pressure to change the law but began the process of redefining who the typical marijuana user was. People began to think that marijuana users were not all crazed monsters who would murder without a moment's hesitation. All of this raised questions about the harmfulness of marijuana. In addition, people began to distinguish among experimenting, occasional use, and heavy use.

While marijuana may have been more acceptable, it was still illegal, and throughout the 1970s arrests continued at the rate of about 400,000 per year, about 90 percent of which were for simple possession (Himmelstein, 1986). And, while penalties were reduced, people were still being penalized. For example, in 1961 the average sentence of imprisonment for those convicted of marijuana violations in the federal courts was just over seventy months. By 1975 this average had dropped to about thirty months (Brown, Flanagan, & McLeod, 1984).

Beginning in 1978, there was a backlash to the efforts to make marijuana more legally and morally acceptable. The federal government completely reversed its stance on marijuana; the New Right became a more powerful political force and made the antimarijuana stance a part of its program; and parent groups began to form to deal with the issue of drugs, including marijuana (Himmelstein, 1986).

Federal Government Reverses Its Stance

In 1977 publications of the DEA deemphasized the importance of the marijuana problem and argued that enforcement was a matter best left to the states. It also suggested that decriminalization might be an option worth considering. By 1980, before the election of Ronald Reagan, the DEA was portraying marijuana as the most serious drug problem facing the United States, requiring a coordinated federal, state, and public effort (Koski & Eckberg, 1983). The White House also shifted its position on marijuana. In 1977 a presidential adviser was urging Congress to decriminalize marijuana in federal laws. By 1979 that adviser's replacement was stressing the growing problem of marijuana use and the importance of federal action (Himmelstein, 1986). The average penalty for convicted marijuana users in federal courts rose from about thirty months in 1975 to over fifty months in 1982 (Brown, Flanagan, & McLeod, 1984).

Rise of the New Right

Some conservatives, such as William F. Buckley, Jr., saw the criminaliz-ation of marijuana as an unnecessary intrusion of government into the lives of citizens. A more vocal group of conservatives, however, moved into power in the late 1970s. In contrast to those taking a libertarian approach, these conservatives were more concerned about the use of marijuana for simple hedonistic pleasure and the possibility that it might have serious harmful effects (Himmelstein, 1986). For them, marijuana use was not simply a practical problem, it was a moral issue.

Rise of Parent Groups

Hundreds of antidrug parent groups rose during this time and included marijuana among the drugs they targeted. In 1980 the National Federation of Parents for Drug Free Youth came into being to unite parent groups throughout the country. These groups focused on antidrug education, stricter policing of schools, and legislation outlawing drug paraphernalia shops. By 1985 the National Federation of Parents for Drug Free Youth was coordinating over 8,000 parent groups in the United States (Lawn, 1985).

Part of the concern was over reports by national surveys that drug use among 12- to 17-year-olds was increasing (from 7 percent in 1972 to 17 percent in 1979). Further, while studies did not generally support the idea that marijuana caused any long-term physical damage, much of the research was inconclusive, and parents were particularly concerned about its effects on growing children (Himmelstein, 1986) and the possibility that young people who used marijuana would be tempted to try other drugs.

The impact of this backlash against marijuana was considerable. In 1977, for example, the National Organization for the Reform of Marijuana Laws (NORML) predicted that by 1979 half of the states would have removed criminal penalties for the possession of marijuana. Since 1977 no additional states have decriminalized marijuana. To the contrary, states have been reinstating criminal penalties. In the late 1980s Oregon reinstituted criminal penalties, leaving Alaska as the only state in which it was legal to possess or cultivate small amounts of marijuana. In November of 1990 voters in Alaska reinstated criminal penalties for marijuana, although officials have suggested the law will not be enforced (Egan, 1991). Nationally, the trend has been to increase rather than reduce penalties. There has been a crackdown on the sale of drug paraphernalia, and a major effort to eradicate domestic production (Himmelstein, 1986). During the 1980s there have also been efforts to categorize as drug paraphernalia (and hence ban) pro-marijuana books and magazines.

Prior to 1981, the DEA's cooperative marijuana eradication programs were limited to Hawaii and California. This effort was expanded during 1981 to include Oregon, Florida, Missouri and Kentucky. In 1982 twenty-five states participated, and this number rose to forty in 1983 (Lawn, 1984). By 1988 all but three states were participating with the DEA in marijuana eradication programs. There has also been a reduction in public support for decriminalization and an increase in the percentage of people who believe the regular use of marijuana is harmful (Johnston, O'Malley, & Bachman, 1986).

In 1969 only 12 percent of Americans thought marijuana should be legalized. By 1977 this had risen to 28 percent but by 1985 had fallen to 23 percent (Gallup, 1985). These figures illustrate that the backlash has been only partial and that there is still no widespread public consensus about the proper legal response to marijuana use and production. For example, there has not been a return to the view that anyone who uses marijuana will become a crazed killer, and there is still a distinction between occasional and heavy use. For many, major concerns with marijuana today are less focused on the effects of the drug and more on the possibility that it is a gateway to the use of other, more dangerous drugs (e.g., Mann, 1985). It was within the context of cultural ambiguity and stepped-up interdiction of foreign marijuana during the 1970s that domestic marijuana production began.

In the 1980s support for legalization continued to wane. During this period the "crack epidemic" heightened public concerns about drugs in general. Other factors that contributed to the erosion of support for legalizing marijuana were a general concern with health and nutrition and with the effects of drugs on employee productivity. During the 1980s the number of tobacco users declined and numerous legal restrictions were enacted to limit the use of tobacco in public areas. At the same time consumers became more concerned with food additives, the quality of drinking water, and other environmental hazards, such as asbestos and radon.

The 1980s also witnessed a large trade imbalance and a shifting domestic economic base, which raised fears about America's ability to compete in a world economy and concerns about worker productivity. One common justification for drug testing has been to identify unproductive and unsafe workers and to either treat or dismiss them. Thus, marijuana has been of particular concern to those who believe that its use leads to an "amotivational syndrome," in which the user loses the motivation to work (Mann, 1985).

These concerns with health and productivity, combined with public concern about the violence associated with the cocaine trade, have made it difficult to sustain widespread public support for easing restrictions against marijuana. Consequently, the 1980s saw a shift toward harsher penalties and more concerted efforts to enforce marijuana laws. It is the law during the 1980s under which growers in this study were operating and to which our attention now turns.

FEDERAL MARIJUANA LAWS IN THE 1980s

In the 1980s, the federal laws dealing with marijuana became more complex and severe. Terms of imprisonment and fines for various offenses were greatly increased and the powers of forfeiture were strengthened as the result of several laws—the Comprehensive Crime Control Act of 1984, the Anti-Drug Abuse Act of 1986, and the Anti-Drug Abuse Amendment Act of 1988. Discussion here focuses primarily on those charges and issues relevant to this research study: manufacture and distribution of marijuana, possession of marijuana, conspiracy, forfeiture, and denial of federal benefits. Because the study concentrates on general trends and principles, some legal distinctions may have been omitted. Also, to simplify the discussion, the penalties described are generally those applied only to first-time offenders (none of the growers in this study had prior arrests for growing); in most cases, penalties are doubled for people with prior offenses. More complete and comprehensive listings of the federal laws (U.S.C. 1982 and 1988, Title 21) are included in Appendix B. These listings also summarize other laws of interest, such as distribution to minors and continuing criminal enterprise.

In the early 1980s the penalties for manufacture of marijuana, distribution of marijuana, or possession of marijuana with intent to manufacture or distribute were up to five years in prison and up to a $15,000 fine for a first offender. If the amount of marijuana exceeded 1,000 pounds, the penalty could go up to fifteen years prison and a $125,000 fine.

By 1988 the laws for manufacture and distribution had become increasingly complex, including clauses which dealt with the cultivation of marijuana on public lands and the use of booby traps. Essentially, four categories of crime were defined, based on weight or number of plants, with each category carrying different penalties. In the least weight category—less than fifty kilograms of a substance containing a detectable amount of marijuana or less than fifty plants—a first offender can receive up to five years in prison and up to a $250,000 fine. If a first offender is convicted in the third weight category (100 kilograms or more or 100 or more plants), a prison sentence of between five and forty years becomes mandatory and fines can be up to $2,000,000. If the weight exceeds 1,000 kilograms or 1,000 plants (the largest weight category), punishment must be between ten years and life imprisonment, with fines up to $4,000,000. Moreover, the terms of imprisonment in these last two categories cannot be suspended, and the offender is ineligible for parole.

The penalties for simple possession or distribution of a small amount of marijuana without remuneration increased also, though not as dramatically. In the early 1980s a first offender could get up to one year in prison and a $5,000 fine, a prior offender up to two years and a $10,000 fine. Currently, a first offender can also get up to one year in prison, but a minimum $1,000 fine is required, with no maximum specified. For a prior drug offender, some prison becomes mandatory (fifteen days to two years for one prior offense, ninety days to three years for two or more priors). Again, minimum fines, with no maximums, are specified.

A major change in the possession laws was the addition of a civil penalty of up to $10,000. As a civil penalty, the law merely requires "clear and convincing proof" rather than the stricter "beyond a reasonable doubt" standard in criminal cases (Marsarak, 1988). Moreover, expungement procedures for first offenders now apply only to individuals assessed civil penalties. Proceedings can be dismissed after three years if it is the first civil penalty, the penalty has been paid, there have been no more drug offenses, and the individual agrees to a drug test that shows he is drug-free. In these cases, a nonpublic record of the disposition is retained solely for the purpose of determining prior offense in case of subsequent charges.

Besides manufacture, distribution, or possession, a person can be charged with conspiracy. The federal law reads: "Any person who attempts or conspires to commit any offense defined in this subchapter shall be subject to the same penalties as those prescribed for the offense, the commission of which was the object of the attempt or conspiracy" (U.S.C. 1988, Title 21, Sec 846). This charge was frequently used in the federal cases included in this study.

Federal forfeiture laws were also strengthened in the 1980s. In 1984 a clause concerning criminal forfeiture was added, where it was stated that any person convicted of a drug violation, punishable by imprisonment for more than one year, shall forfeit any property (1) derived from any proceeds the person obtained as the result of such violation or (2) that was used, or intended to be used, to commit the violation. More significant, and more useful to prosecutors, was the strengthening of civil forfeiture laws (Sinoway, 1987). Added to the list of items that could be forfeited was "all real property, including any right, title, and interest in the whole of any lot or tract of land" (U.S.C. 1988, Title 21, Sec 881(a)(7)) that was used or intended to be used to commit a drug violation punishable by more than one year's imprisonment. Thus, it appears that a first offender could not have his or her house or land forfeited for simple possession, but it would be possible in all other cases.

Finally, another significant introduction was the denial of federal benefits to any person convicted of distribution or possession. These include the issuance of any grant, contract, loan, professional or commercial license, with the length of denial dependent on the type of offense and history of prior offenses. For farmers, this penalty includes many of the subsidy programs sponsored by the Federal government.

In practice, of the fourteen resolved federal cases in this study, only one did *not* result in a prison sentence, and in most cases no fine was assessed. Sentences varied from six months to ten years, with a median sentence of four years. However, only four of these cases occurred after major changes in the law, so whether the federal government will actually utilize the maximums now allowed remains to be seen.

ILLINOIS MARIJUANA LAWS IN THE 1980s

In Illinois, the primary location of this study, state penalties and fines are not as large as those on the federal level, and changes have not been as extensive in the 1980s. In 1987 the law was changed so that the number of plants could be used as a criterion for deciding the seriousness of charges, instead of using only weight, and in 1989 a new charge was introduced called "cannabis trafficking." Again the discussion focuses on the most common charges.

The penalties in Illinois for manufacturing, delivery, possession, and cultivation vary by weight and number of plants. For manufacture or delivery, or possession with intent to manufacture or deliver, greater than 500 grams of a substance containing marijuana (the largest weight category), a first-time offender can be sentenced to from three to seven years and fined a maximum of $100,000. These penalties also apply for cultivation or possession of greater than fifty cannabis sativa plants. For simple possession of greater than 500 grams of a substance containing marijuana (again, the largest weight category), a first-time offender can be sentenced to two to five years and fined a maximum of $10,000. For any of these charges mitigating factors allow for probation, periodic imprisonment, or a conditional discharge.

While the limits of the fines in Illinois are lower than those of the federal government, the state can add to a fine the street value of the marijuana confiscated. This provision can considerably increase the total fine levied. In two state-level cases in this study, this clause was used to fine the participants more than $100,000.

Illinois law allows a "first offender's probation," which is more flexible and inclusive than the federal law permits. First offender's probation is allowed for first-time drug offenders found guilty of manufacturing, delivery, possession of less than thirty grams of cannabis, or of cultivation or possession of cannabis plants. Under this provision, after successful completion of probation, charges are dismissed against the individual and kept only for purposes of determining prior offense, if a subsequent offense is committed.

Illinois law also has a conspiracy clause, but it is more restrictive than federal law. To be charged with calculated criminal cannabis conspiracy, the offender must be acting with at least two other people, have more than thirty grams or twenty plants, hold an organizational position, or have obtained more than $500 from the enterprise. First offenders receive mandatory sentences of three to seven years and fines of up to $200,000.

Like the federal government, state forfeiture laws allow the seizure of all substances containing cannabis, all new materials, products, and equipment used in connection with cannabis, conveyances used to transport cannabis (with certain exceptions), and all money, things of value, books, and records used in violation of the act. With respect to property, the law is worded differently. Property can be seized if there is probable cause to believe it is "directly or indirectly dangerous to health or safety" or in "accordance with the Code of Criminal Procedure of 1963" (Illinois Revised Statutes, Chapter 56 1/2, Sec 12). One reason often cited for moving a case from the state to the federal level was to make the seizure of property easier. However, the only two clear cases of confiscation of property of which we have information occurred on the state level. In one federal case, where the farmer was hopelessly in debt, the farmer agreed to turn over his farm to the Farmers Home Administration (FmHA) as part of his sentence. In turn, the FmHA allowed the farmer to rent the property.

Of the forty-eight state-level cases in this study, about one-third resulted in prison sentences. These sentences varied from one month to five years, with 75 percent sentenced to two years or less. One person did receive an eight-year sentence, but this was the result of an armed-violence charge, and not for charges relating to marijuana. At the state level, fines varied tremendously and showed little correlation with the number of plants grown. Some counties simply fined more heavily than others. For example, in one county a person was given an $88,000 fine for growing fifty plants; in another county, the fine was $3,000 for growing 429 plants. These extremes show the large amount of discretion available to the court in assessing fines.

The differences between federal and state sentencing practices may not be as large as they seem. Most of the very large cases, where a large number of plants were involved, were handled on the federal level. Also, offenders may serve only a third of a federal sentence, compared to half for a state sentence. However, given the large maximums now allowed on the federal level, marijuana offenders would probably prefer to be prosecuted on the state level. Given the same offense, sentences are likely to be lighter and probation (including first-offender's probation) more probable at the state level. For example, in one federal case, a first-time offender growing twenty-five plants was given eighteen months in prison; similar cases on the state level resulted in a one-year term of first offender's probation for the defendants.

When can the federal government prosecute a marijuana-growing case? Obviously, the federal government prosecutes if the growing is on federal land, such as national forests, or when the case has interstate connections; in actuality, the federal government can intervene any time it chooses. Section 801 of Title 21, U.S.C. 1988, states:

> Controlled substances manufactured and distributed intrastate cannot be differentiated from controlled substances manufactured and distributed interstate. . . . Federal control of the intrastate incidents of the traffic in controlled substances is essential to the effective control of the interstate incidents of such traffic.

In one case, the federal government intervened when it felt the defendants had been punished too lightly by the state. Three of the four defendants were retried (the fourth was exempted by cooperating with the federal government), and two were given four-year prison terms, where previously they had been given fines and probation by the state. While this occurrence is highly unusual, it shows the discretion the federal government has in pursuing drug cases.

Clearly, some discretion is necessary in the law to allow for mitigating and aggravating factors. While there should be more uniformity in the assessment of fines in Illinois, prison terms are specified with reasonable ranges and options. On the federal level, the possible ranges are overwhelming. Most likely, a first offender growing 100 plants and faced with a charge of possession with intent to distribute (a common charge) would receive the minimum five-year sentence. But if a judge chose to be punitive and to set an example, the defendant could legally be sentenced to forty years.

SUMMARY

Since its national ban in 1937, the legal status of marijuana has fluctuated dramatically over time and across jurisdictions. Penalties have ranged from citations to lengthy prison sentences. During the 1980s, the time covered by this study, both federal and state laws against the production of marijuana became more harsh. Though some may see marijuana as a minor drug compared with cocaine or heroin, both state and federal law treat growing marijuana, particularly in large amounts, as a very serious offense. In the 1980s and early 1990s there was nothing "minor" or "casual" about the potential consequences of a conviction for cultivating marijuana.

4

THE RISE OF THE DOMESTIC MARIJUANA INDUSTRY

Just as marijuana use did not become widespread throughout U.S. society until the 1960s, domestic production did not become an important factor until the 1970s. In·the 1980s the popularity of domestic cultivation continued at an accelerated pace. Because marijuana production is a clandestine activity, no one can fully know how much marijuana is grown or how many people are involved. Further, estimates vary widely depending upon the source. Though imprecise, these estimates are among the only starting points in outlining the extent of domestic cultivation.

HOW MUCH MARIJUANA IS GROWN?

For the late 1980s most estimates of the percentage of domestically grown marijuana used in the United States ranged from 25 percent to 50 percent (Slaughter, 1988; Gettman, 1987). A common technique for making these estimates is to assume that from 10 to 20 percent of the marijuana available in the United States is seized and then extrapolate from seizure figures. This approach, of course, cannot take into account such factors as changing law-enforcement priorities and changes in public attitudes toward reporting drug suspects to the police. Two examples illustrate the difficulty of making estimates of domestic and foreign marijuana production. The first is a 1982 DEA report that admitted that in the previous year 38 percent more domestic marijuana was *seized* than was *previously believed to exist* (cited in Warner, 1986).

Second, and even more revealing, are figures for 1989, which show a 20 percent *increase* in estimated domestic production compared with 1988, while the domestic industry's share of the total estimated U.S. marijuana supply dropped from 25 percent to 10 percent. This odd combination of figures is explained by a dramatic increase in the estimated production figures for Mexico, which increased from 4,700 metric tons in 1988 to 42,200 metric tons in 1990—a nine-fold increase in one year. Illustrating how fickle these estimations are, this increase is entirely the result of new monitoring techniques rather than a perceived increase in production (NNICC, 1990). In 1989 the United States began using satellite information to determine the size of Mexico's marijuana crop. The approach is controversial and may give an exaggerated image of accuracy ("U.S. Says Mexico's Production of Marijuana Was Underestimated," 1990). Satellite data cannot, for example, differentiate marijuana cultivation for harvest from that which grows wild, an issue discussed in chapter 5. Use of this technology also highlights the political sensitivity of drug enforcement. If it is possible to precisely locate and count marijuana plants in Mexico, only political factors can explain why this technology is not used in the United States to locate plants for eradication.

In estimating the extent of marijuana *use*, Kleiman (1989) has criticized seizure-based estimates in favor of estimates extrapolated from random surveys of households. Unfortunately, for estimating domestic *production*, there are no alternatives that provide even a marginal improvement over seizure-based figures.

Precisely estimating the size of the marijuana crop is an impossible task. However, even the most conservative estimates suggest that domestic production accounts for a substantial share of the domestic market. Further, most observers (from both sides of the issue) seem to agree that domestic production is increasing. The National Narcotics Intelligence Consumers Committee (NNICC), for example, estimated that in 1984 domestic marijuana comprised about 12 percent of the total U.S. supply. Table 4.1 shows that by 1988 this figure had risen to 25 percent (NNICC, 1988). Perhaps more important than its contribution relative to imported marijuana is the total estimated volume of domestic marijuana and its potency. By any indicator, the domestic industry is large and production is increasing.

These production estimates are particularly noteworthy when juxtaposed with survey data showing that the number of users and the amount of marijuana they use have gone down since 1979 (see chapter 2). In addition, since much of the domestic marijuana is high-grade sinsemilla, which is as much as three times the potency of commercial foreign marijuana, a metric ton of domestic sinsemilla might well displace as much as three metric tons of imported commercial-grade marijuana. (See chapter 5 for a discussion of sinsemilla and marijuana potency.)

The importance of considering both weight and potency when assessing domestic marijuana's share of the market is illustrated by Kleiman (1989), using 1986 figures:

Table 4.1
Estimated Domestic Marijuana Production, 1982–1989 in Metric Tons

				YEAR				
	1982	1983	1984	1985	1986	1987	1988	1989
Domestic	2,000	2,000	2,000	2,100	2,100	3,250	4,600	5,500
Total	13,215	14,300	13,725	10,850	11,550	13,065	18,420	54,281
Percent Domestic	15%	14%	12%	19%	18%	25%	25%	10%

Source: NNICC, 1984; 1987; 1988; 1989.

Note: Where ranges were given, the midpoint was selected. Total includes marijuana seized by officials.

If, very roughly, domestic marijuana consists of two-thirds
high-potency marijuana averaging slightly less than three times
normal potency, domestic marijuana would account for close
to 30 percent—rather than 18 percent—of the effective volume
of marijuana intoxication. This contribution would not be
reflected in an analysis based on drug volumes or usage
frequency. (41)

In short, the precise volume of marijuana produced domestically is
unknown, but the volume is substantial and estimates based solely on weight or
number of plants considerably understate the contribution of the domestic
industry to the total supply of domestic marijuana. Further, there are no
forecasters who see the domestic industry as occupying a shrinking portion of
the total marijuana market.

In describing the domestic marijuana market, one can speak, not only
in terms of its absolute value, but also in terms of its size relative to other
legitimate agricultural crops. It is sometimes said that marijuana is the first-,
second-, or third-largest cash crop. While the veracity of this assertion can
never be proven, one can utilize existing data to determine whether such claims
are at least within the realm of possibility.

Estimating the value of the total marijuana crop depends on a series
of assumptions about the percentage of all marijuana seized, the amount of
marijuana that is sinsemilla, as opposed to commercial grade, and the amount
of wild marijuana that is harvested and sold at a very low price. Estimates of
seizures for drugs of all kinds typically range from 10 to 20 percent. That is,
it is commonly believed that each year law enforcement seizes between 10 and
20 percent of available illicit drugs in the United States. For marijuana the
problem is compounded by changing growing strategies, which make detection
more difficult and which provide incentives to grow more potent (and hence
more valuable) marijuana, and the simultaneous increase in law-enforcement
effort, which makes detection more likely. How these various forces balance
out is anyone's guess. Consequently, the following analysis presents two
estimates, one based on the assumption that 20 percent of cultivated marijuana
is seized and the other on the assumption that only 10 percent is seized.
Regarding price, it is assumed that the typical cultivated plant is worth
approximately $1,000. While many cultivated plants will yield more than this,
others will die before harvest or yield relatively little. Some growers in this
study thought the $1,000 figure too high, while others thought it too low. This
price, however, is consistent with figures used by officials and is within the
range given by interviewed growers.

Using this set of procedures, marijuana seizure data for 1988 and 1989
were averaged to give some adjustment for yearly fluctuations. During this
period, an average of 6,482,233 cultivated plants were eradicated. Assuming
that seizures represent 20 percent of the total crop and that plants are worth

approximately $1,000 each, the cash value of marijuana for this period is $32,411,165,000—over $32 billion. If it is assumed that seizures represent 10 percent of the total crop, the average cash value of marijuana in 1988–89 is double that, or nearly $65 billion. Table 4.2 shows that when compared with the average value of the top five legitimate agricultural crops for 1988–89, marijuana is far and away more valuable. In fact, for marijuana to equal the value of corn, the largest legitimate cash crop, one would have to assume that law enforcement seizes 44 percent of all cultivated marijuana each year. This seizure rate, incidentally, is approximately that estimated by the NNICC (1989) but is much higher than most estimates. The differences between marijuana and legitimate crops are even more striking when one considers that a substantially greater proportion of the cash value of marijuana is clear profit and the income is generally tax-free.

Table 4.2
Value of Marijuana and Other Cash Crops for 1988–1989

Crop	Average Value for 1988-89 in 1000s
Marijuana (10% seizure)	$64,822,330
Marijuana (20% seizure)	32,411,165
Corn	14,840,542
Hay	11,117,902
Soybeans	11,054,639
Wheat	7,213,088
Cotton	4,071,848

Sources: NNICC, 1989; U.S. Dept. of Agriculture, 1990.

As with seizure figures upon which these computations are based, caution should be exercised in putting too much faith in the precise dollar amounts reported in Table 4.2. However, even if the most conservative estimate (20 percent seizure) is off by more than a factor of two, marijuana would still be the largest cash crop in the United States.

WHERE IS MARIJUANA GROWN IN THE UNITED STATES?

Government data on marijuana seizures also provide a glimpse of *where* marijuana is grown in the United States. The 1990 Domestic Cannabis Eradication Program ranks states by the number of cultivated plants seized. These figures are presented in Table 4.3. One should not make too much of

the precise ranking of individual states since these rankings change somewhat
from year to year, partly because marijuana is easy to grow and there are
varieties suitable for a range of environments. Thus, commercial growers who
feel pressure in one state may simply move elsewhere the next year. Kleiman
(1989) uses a similar argument to account for the ever-changing ranking of
foreign suppliers of marijuana.

Table 4.3
**1990 Domestic Cannabis Eradication/Suppression Program, Cultivated
Plants Eradicated**

1. Missouri	1,141,687	26. West Virginia	25,350
2. Oklahoma	1,013,036	27. Arizona	24,760
3. Nebraska	760,523	28. South Carolina	23,636
4. Hawaii	752,937	29. Kansas	18,289
5. Kentucky	616,289	30. Maine	13,729
6. Tennessee	542,580	31. Iowa	12,027
7. Michigan	311,206	32. South Dakota	10,774
8. Illinois	288,167	33. Alaska	8,637
9. California	199,105	34. Vermont	5,585
10. Alabama	192,918	35. New Mexico	4,447
11. Minnesota	187,349	36. New York	4,283
12. Indiana	187,107	37. Colorado	3,846
13. North Carolina	145,916	38. Montana	3,730
14. Arkansas	125,420	39. Massachusetts	3,444
15. Wisconsin	107,940	40. Idaho	3,194
16. Georgia	97,233	41. Maryland	2,886
17. Florida	92,901	42. New Hampshire	2,542
18. Texas	69,865	43. Nevada	2,200
19. Oregon	59,785	44. North Dakota	1,761
20. Mississippi	53,066	45. Utah	1,582
21. Pennsylvania	51,673	46. Wyoming	1,291
22. Louisiana	44,596	47. New Jersey	526
23. Ohio	43,437	48. Rhode Island	500
24. Virginia	33,660	49. Connecticut	326
25. Washington	30,801	50. Delaware	227

Source: DEA, 1990.

Year-to-year fluctuations in the ranking of states are probably even
more influenced by law-enforcement resources and simple luck. As an
example, in 1987 Illinois reported eradicating nearly 32,000 cultivated plants,
and in 1988 this figure dropped to just over 9,000 plants. In 1989, however, a

Figure 4.1
Fifteen States with the Most Cultivated Marijuana Eradications in 1990

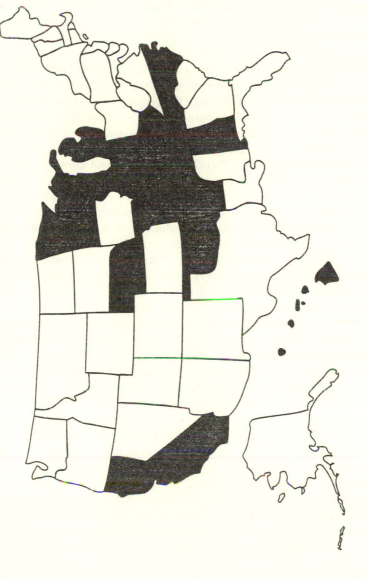

Source: Data are drawn from the DEA, 1990.

single operation was discovered with more than 58,000 plants, and in 1990 288,000 plants were eradicated in Illinois. Thus, annual fluctuations are sometimes considerable, and discovering (or missing) even one or two very large operations can dramatically alter the annual figures for a single state.

At the same time, several states, including Hawaii, Kentucky, Tennessee, Missouri, California, and Alabama consistently report high seizures. In 1990, for example, four states (Missouri, Oklahoma, Nebraska, and Hawaii) accounted for over half of all cultivated marijuana eradicated in the United States (DEA, 1990). One feature of these rankings over time is that, as a group, midwestern states typically make the largest contribution to the domestic marijuana supply, as shown in Figure 4.1. It is also important to note that marijuana cultivation is not a phenomenon isolated to one or two states but is practiced throughout the country.

The folk belief in the 1960s that marijuana will grow only in hot, arid environments, such as Mexico, is as erroneous as the belief that coca bushes can be cultivated only on mountaintops. Further, the rise of indoor cultivation makes outdoor climate largely irrelevant and urban growing more practical.

Marijuana is also cultivated on federal land and has been a particularly visible issue in the National Forest System. In 1989, nearly 429,000 cultivated cannabis plants were eradicated in the National Forest System from 4,108 cultivation sites (Forest Service, 1989). Compared with 1988 this is a 21 percent increase in plants eradicated and a 68 percent increase over 1987, when 255,000 plants were eradicated.

Just as marijuana cultivation is not evenly distributed among states, it is not evenly distributed among national forests. In 1989, for example, the Daniel Boone National Forest in Kentucky accounted for over one-third of the plants eradicated in the National Forest System (Forest Service, 1989).

Much has been made in the press of the violence associated with marijuana growing in the National Forests (e.g., Wolkomir & Wolkomir, 1988; "Violent Gardeners," 1986; McHugh, 1986; Shabecoff, 1986; "Rise in Marijuana Cultivation," 1984). Each year the forest service "significantly constrains" (i.e., closes off) thousands of acres of land because of the potential for violence by marijuana growers. The precise nature of the association between marijuana growing and violence in the national forests is neither direct nor obvious, however. For example, between 1987 and 1989 the number of cultivated marijuana plants eradicated *rose 68 percent*, but the number of acres declared significantly constrained *declined 53 percent*, from 722,000 acres to 338,000 acres (Forest Service, 1988; 1989). And, while the number of booby-trapped sites nearly doubled from 1987 to 1989 (from 31 to 57), they still represent just over 1 percent of all sites. Further, injuries from booby traps dropped from two in 1987 to zero in 1989, suggesting most traps were not lethal or were set up in plain sight as visible deterrents rather than carefully concealed to produce surprise and maximum harm.

Growing on federal land makes it more difficult for the police to tie a patch to a particular grower. For growers, this advantage must be weighed against the increased likelihood that the patch will be discovered (and either robbed or reported to authorities) by hikers or hunters. In addition, arrests for growing marijuana on federal land will lead to federal drug charges, which are often more harsh than those brought at the state level (see chapter 3).

HOW MANY PEOPLE ARE GROWING MARIJUANA?

Because domestic marijuana cultivation is a recent phenomenon that often occurs outside the urban settings of most drug studies, little is known about the industry. This neglect is particularly striking given the large number of people involved. In 1986 the federal government estimated there were between 90,000 and 150,000 commercial growers in the United States and over 1 million people who grew for personal use (cited in Gettman, 1987). The National Organization for the Reform of Marijuana Laws (NORML) calculated the number of growers by combining overall crop production estimates with a projection of the amount that typical growers produce in a year (five pounds for personal-use growers and thirteen pounds for commercial growers). Using this approach, NORML estimated there were approximately 250,000 commercial growers and over 2 million personal-use growers in 1986 (Gettman, 1987). If these latter figures are correct, the arrest and imprisonment of all *commercial growers alone* would result in a 50 percent increase in the federal prison population, assuming there has been no continued increase in the number of growers since 1986.

As is true with estimating crops, estimating the number of growers is nearly impossible. Many plots are seized each year with no arrest. For example, the Domestic Cannabis Eradication/Suppression Program report by the DEA indicates that during 1990 law-enforcement officers eradicated 29,469 plots of marijuana which contained a total of 125,876,752 plants. These eradications led to only 5,729 arrests in 1990, or a ratio of five plots per arrestee or 22,000 plants per arrestee (DEA, 1990). If only *cultivated* plants are included, there are approximately 1,280 plants eradicated per arrestee. The matter is complicated by the fact that it is currently impossible to know the extent to which individual growers have multiple plots or to which plots are tended by multiple growers. Further, the smallest operations are least likely to be discovered by police. Using seizures to approximate production may therefore significantly underrepresent small-scale growers, who may constitute the largest category of producers.

WHO ARE THE GROWERS?

While the government has been willing to hazard guesses on the number of growers and the volume of production, there have been no corresponding efforts to identify or monitor changes in characteristics of the grower population. A 1984 DEA report recognized that marijuana growers may be drawn from all walks of life and may not fit media images of drug dealers:

> All types of individuals are involved in domestic marijuana cultivation, ranging from seasoned drug traffickers to white collar business executives. Farmers, who generally are economically hard pressed, are cultivating marijuana in addition to corn or wheat to meet financial obligations and satisfy debts. Persons who are unemployed or senior citizens who can't live off retirement benefits are selling marijuana as an alternative source of income. Successful business executives are financing marijuana cultivation as another form of investment. Domestic marijuana cultivation has become an integral part of the economy in depressed areas of southeastern Oklahoma and northern California. (quoted in Slaughter, 1988:460)

One objective of this study was to develop a description of growers and to suggest questions that might be used in later studies to make comparisons across time and location.

Less glamorous than smugglers, less visible than street addicts, and working with a "soft" drug, marijuana growers have received relatively little attention in the professional and popular literature. In the absence of routinely collected systematic data on growers, it was necessary to rely on journalistic accounts as a starting point.

Most reports focus on growers in northern California, although in 1989 and 1990 there were several descriptions of growers in Kentucky (Jehl, 1990; Johnson, 1989). California growers have been described by Raphael (1985), Warner (1986), and Chapple (1984). In addition, Boyle's 1984 novel *Budding Prospects* presents a description of California growers with considerable (and credible) detail about the process and people involved.

Although most of Warner's efforts were directed at marijuana smugglers, he did spend time among growers and notes that the very nature of marijuana growing involves a different type of individual than marijuana smuggling:

> Marijuana growing is land-bound. It is an ample but slow buck, dependent on a plant cycle. People don't drift in and out of growing marijuana as much as they do in smuggling. If they make money from their first crop without being traumatized, they tend to stay with it for a few years, changing their garden sites, changing their techniques and their partners, but still enmeshed in the cycle of putting seeds in the ground and waiting for the harvest.
>
> Like smuggling, something resembling an 80–20 rule seems to hold for marijuana growing. That is, the majority, maybe 80 percent of the growers, produce a minority of the domestically grown marijuana, maybe 20 percent, using ballpark figures. (Warner, 1986:200)

The focus of this study is not on the 80 percent who grow only a few plants for home consumption and to share with friends. Many of the individuals written about in such magazines as *High Times* approach growing as a "hobby." Although these popular accounts are insightful and proved to be excellent starting points for the present study, they do not provide enough information to demonstrate the existence of clear patterns among growers. Our attention is therefore on those who raise marijuana primarily for profit; that is, for whom marijuana production is a business.

TYPES OF GROWERS

The growers described by popular literature and journalistic accounts illustrate the variety of individuals and motivating factors in marijuana growing. This literature, combined with interviews conducted for this study, led to the development of a typology of growers (Weisheit, 1990; 1991a). This typology went through a series of revisions as interviews were conducted and new cases were discovered. It has proven to be a useful way of categorizing growers in most regions of the United States, although the proportion of growers fitting into a particular type seems to vary from one region to the next. Finally, it is important to recognize that these are broad theoretical types, intended to facilitate clearer thinking about the issue. Many growers primarily fit into one type but have some traits from one or both of the two remaining types.

The Hustler

This type of marijuana grower is an entrepreneur by instinct. Hustlers may have used marijuana and may have engaged in some dealing for the challenge of it, but neither activity is a necessary prerequisite for their involvement in marijuana growing. Marijuana growing is appealing as a business challenge, and for some the risks associated with growing are part of the appeal. Although the money they make may serve as some indication of success, they are generally less motivated by the money itself than by the challenge of being a successful entrepreneur. They could just have easily set up business in any one of a dozen legitimate or illegitimate enterprises, and once the thrill wears off, they are likely to move out of marijuana growing. Although some may be involved in the day-to-day process of growing, they may also serve as brokers, providing front money, technical assistance, and the "brains" to run the operation.

The literature presents several examples of this type of grower. A Texas case involving a "short, chunky, balding, 63-year-old farmer and one of the best-known businessmen in town" (Applebome, 1985) is one example. The farmer, Skinner Brown, was a lifelong resident of a Texas community of only 7,500:

> After inheriting some land, he spent much of his time diligently buying up more and more. . . . He was an agricultural entrepreneur. . . . He owned the local feed store, S and B Chemicals, and always seemed interested in ways to expand its scope. Not long ago he began selling satellite dishes, along with hog pellets and sheep manure. He continued to buy up land, leveraging himself to the hilt to do it. At the time of his arrest he owned almost five thousand acres. (10)

In his novel *Budding Prospects*, Boyle's character Vogelsang is another example of a hustler. He had a variety of investments, some legal and some not, and saw marijuana growing as simply another way to make quick money. He fronted money for the operation but had little to do with the day-to-day labor of caring for the plants. Aside from his "investment" in marijuana, he financed the refurbishing of Victorian houses, traded stock on which he had good (i.e., inside) information, and was involved in land speculation.

Among growers, it is unlikely that the number of hustlers is very large. Their contribution to the domestic industry is likely to be considerable, however. For one thing, their interest in success generally means their operations will be large and will expand substantially over time if given the chance. For another, their "business" contacts and the size of their operations encourage them to develop networks for moving and marketing domestic marijuana, or to take advantage of existing networks. Their ability to bring people together and organize them means that hustlers have the potential for strengthening networks that may continue long after they are gone.

The current study includes two such entrepreneurs. At the time of his arrest the first had the largest marijuana crop ever seized in Illinois, as well as the largest fine ever imposed on an arrested grower. He seemed proud of these facts, holding them up as evidence of the scale of his operation. At the time of his arrest he told the sheriff that he (the sheriff) should be grateful because closing an operation the size of his would likely guarantee his reelection. While in prison he studied horticulture. Following his release, he wrote a book on marijuana growing and served as a paid consultant to those interested in "organic gardening." He agreed to be interviewed for the study only after renegotiating the standard fee paid interview subjects.

A second case fit this category, although no interview was conducted. The individual had contracted with several others to grow very large marijuana plots on their farms. He provided the seeds and technical expertise and made provisions for marketing the crop. He had planned to expand at least one of the operations to as many as 30,000 plants. At the time of the study he was a fugitive from the police (the farmers having been arrested) and his whereabouts were unknown.

The Pragmatist

The pragmatist enters the marijuana business out of economic necessity and approaches the activity with no moral or philosophical righteousness. This individual would rather not be in the marijuana business but feels there are few options available to relieve his or her economic problems. Unlike the hustler, the pragmatist is in the marijuana business to help cope with tough economic times, not to become wealthy. Several growers in this study were pragmatists:

G04:   I didn't plan on getting rich or anything, I just wanted to hang on to what I had. I had no illusions of buying a yacht or anything like that. I was just trying to hang on to what I had . . . I believe most of the people who are trying to make money off of marijuana are doing it because they're broke. And, they are usually like me, I was faced with foreclosure, even though I was not a farmer. A lot of the farmers round here, you know, lose 10 to 15 thousand a year growing corn and make it up growing reefer.

G29:   I was laid off at the coal mine, and hell, had house payments and everything else coming in. And, I just couldn't make it farming and stuff, and I couldn't find a job. So I thought I'd try that [marijuana growing] first.

For some, growing marijuana offered them a chance to start over financially and in the process gave them self-confidence:

G09:   I was kinda worried about it [growing]. But, I felt you gotta
         do what you gotta do. There was no work. I couldn't get
         work, and I had a kid to feed. I figure if I'm gonna do it, I'm
         just gonna go all the way and after one year I won't have all
         the paranoia. Nobody can imagine. I mean, I'd go for weeks
         without sleep and that. I wasn't thinking straight. I got too
         involved. I saw that it might take you out of poverty, and you
         know, for a while I did pretty well. I was making more money
         than I had made at anything else, and for the first time in my
         life, I was gaining self-esteem and pride in something I'd
         done, no matter what. I made or broke myself. I didn't have
         to depend on someone else, everything I did was me. That
         built up self-esteem. When I first got into it, it was in '82,
         when the recession was on. There was just no work at all, I
         was just really down. Then I finally had that one year and it
         kept us eating, kept heat in the house and the car, and so that
         automatically changes your whole viewpoint toward things,
         cause I didn't want to sell. I was totally against it, and that
         kinda changes your viewpoint towards things. Even that time
         when I was selling, I had a lot of reservations about that,
         especially after I started growing real high powerful stuff.

Although they may use marijuana, not all do. A grower in this study
said he had an allergic reaction when he used marijuana, and so he never
smoked it. One of Warner's marijuana growers described himself and his wife
as staunch Republicans who had never even tried marijuana. He had punched
out his son for smoking marijuana six or seven years earlier but now used his
son's help in growing it. He described his feelings about marijuana and himself
as a grower in these terms (1986):

         I don't even consider [smoking] it. I'm not going to fry my
         brains. . . . I'm just involved in producing a saleable product.
         I'm just trying to make money. . . . I'm antimarijuana . . . I
         feel that marijuana is destroying young people by changing
         their attitudes about working. I feel so strongly about that
         I'm almost ashamed of growing it. . . . The only way I can
         justify it is that anyone who's gonna smoke it is just gonna
         smoke it, regardless of what I do. (229)

Chapple's (1984) description of California marijuana growers also
contains examples of pragmatists. For example, one woman in his account
grew only seven plants, the quantity she calculated she would need to make
between $5,000 and $10,000 a year—enough for her to get by and keep up on
her modest home and land payments.

Reports from Kentucky suggest that in counties where most of the growing for profit takes place, as many as 40 percent of the growers do not themselves use marijuana, and growing is generally attributed to desparate economic circumstances (Potter, Gaines, & Holbrook, 1989; Jehl, 1990; Johnson, 1989). Pragmatists demonstrate that growing marijuana for profit requires no commitment to a drug lifestyle or even a "liberal" or tolerant attitude toward drugs in general.

The Communal Grower

Communal growers probably represent the single largest category of grower, although their operations are often very small.   They cultivate marijuana as part of a larger lifestyle in which marijuana plays a part. Nearly all of these growers begin as marijuana users and start growing for their own consumption, either to defray the costs of their habit or as a hobby. Unlike the hustler, who is almost a caricature of the true American capitalist, the business side of marijuana growing is of only secondary interest to the communal grower. Economic necessity may push them to grow larger crops, but if these economic problems pass, they are likely to scale back their operations and continue growing for themselves and their friends. A few of these communal growers are holdovers from the late 1960s and early 1970s, but more commonly they are indistinguishable from "ordinary" citizens. For many in this category growing marijuana is also a personal statement of independence or rebellion.

Although some of these individuals gradually drift into large-scale production, most have more modest goals. As Warner (1986) has observed:

> Many of them are motivated as much by ideas of self-suffi-
> ciency (the satisfaction of growing their own) or thrift (not
> having to buy pot) as by making money selling their extra
> ounces or pounds. What money they make seems to go to a
> few purchases they could not afford otherwise, and to good
> times. (200)

Given their approach to the process, communal growers also tend to be more flexible about the price they demand for their marijuana crop, commonly selling it to friends for well below market price. Several growers in this study illustrate this group:

G07:   I probably grew about 10 to 15 pounds per year and about
         three of those pounds were for me personally. Another 4 to
         5 I would give away, and I'd save 5 pounds every year and
         around Christmas time I sold it to the same guy every year,
         and I used that money to buy presents, something we couldn't

otherwise afford. . . . I sold it well under commercial prices. Because you see, that's one of the main reasons I got into it in the first place, because commercial prices were ridiculous, and plus I don't believe in supporting organized crime that's into all this other shit, too. There's a philosophical argument about smoking marijuana that could go on for days, but personally I think it's a person's—if somebody wants to, it's no big deal, if you are an adult. I don't think kids should, of course, but I think if you are an adult and you want to, it's no different than drinking a beer or whiskey or wine, or whatever else. And, it's none of the damn state's business.

Q: You weren't growing mainly for profit then?
G21:   No, no. Not really. Most of what I sold, I sold because people nagged me for it.
Q: Mostly friends?
G21:   Yeah. My friends nagged me for it so much. I'd turn them on to some and then they'd want some, you know. I usually gave in and would sell them some. I gave away a lot. If I was in it for the money I would have sold all that I could, but I gave away a lot.

The idea of simply giving away marijuana is common among communal growers but would be unthinkable for the hustler, unless it was to attract future business. Several communal growers also saw their activities as having political and economic implications. They felt that domestic marijuana growing helped the overall balance of trade with other countries, benefited the local economy, and kept money from going to organized crime, an outcome which they were certain would happen if they bought marijuana through an importer.

G21:   See, my reasons behind growing were monetary, but just for the sake of not having to spend money that I worked for on pot. But there were a lot of other reasons involved. I liked to keep my money in the locality where I live. I considered going across the river to shop, but I didn't. I shop in my own county. Another reason was that I didn't like supporting the black market. Most of the pot or drugs you pay for goes up to Chicago and from Chicago who knows where it goes. You know, a lot of it goes to foreign countries. I just felt I was helping the current [economic] problem rather than hurting society, because I happened to keep the demand [for foreign marijuana] smaller. And, if I support myself, I didn't have to rely on foreign sources.

These economic and political issues were secondary considerations and may have been nothing more than rationalizations to justify their illegal activities to themselves. Nevertheless, these arguments cannot be dismissed as irrelevant to the process if the growers truly believed them, and it appeared they did.

Approaching production as they do, communal growers view other growers as kindred spirits rather than threatening competitors. When communal growers get together, they enjoy sharing experiences and technical information about growing and "war stories" about their brushes with the law and with marijuana thieves. Similarly, this group is less likely to engage in the violence sometimes associated with marijuana growing, such as setting booby traps and guarding crops with automatic weapons or dogs (Lawren, 1985; Warner, 1986; Raphael, 1985).

FOREIGN POLICY AND DOMESTIC MARIJUANA PRODUCTION

It is possible that widespread domestic consumption, combined with the ease with which the hemp plant can be grown, made domestic production inevitable. However, three U.S. foreign policy initiatives in the late 1960s and early 1970s appear to have worked in combination to hasten the increase in domestic production. These were: (1) the U.S.–Mexican border interdiction program known as Operation Intercept in 1969; (2) the U.S. government's cooperative agreement with Mexico to spray marijuana plants there with the herbicide paraquat in 1975; and (3) the Vietnam war.

The relative contribution of each initiative to the rise of domestic marijuana production will probably never be fully known. Points 1 and 2, in particular, represent classic examples of how well-intended drug policies may have unintended consequences. As Peter Reuter of the RAND Corporation has put it, "This is the rare instance in which trade protectionism really worked" (Passell, 1989).

Operation Intercept

On Sunday, September 21, 1969 at 2:30 P.M., Operation Intercept was begun to halt the flow of drugs across the Mexican border. The operation was aimed at stopping all drugs but mainly targeted marijuana and was timed to stop shipment of the fall harvest of marijuana from Mexico (Gooberman, 1974; Brecher, 1972).

The project was enormous, covering the entire 2,500-mile-long border between the United States and Mexico. It was the largest peacetime search-and-seizure operation by civil authorities in history, using the services of more than 2,000 agents. Even so, they simply did not have the manpower to do the job. Within an hour after the operation began, traffic was backed up for more than two-and-a-half miles at some of the thirty-one border-crossing stations. In the first week of the operation, 1,824 border-crossers were strip searched, but this still left some 1,987,000 people who crossed with little or no search. During the first week only thirty-three arrests were made. Similarly, before the operation a usual inspection of vehicles was one minute per vehicle. During the operation this was expanded only to an average of from two to three minutes per vehicle.

It is impossible to know how many shipments were simply never made for fear of being caught. We do know, however, that before the operation an average of 150 pounds of marijuana was seized per day—and that figure was unchanged during the operation. It is also impossible to know how much of the shortage of marijuana in the United States was due to the operation and how much was due to two other important factors: (1) Mexico had been in a drought that summer and less marijuana had been produced, and (2) the demand for marijuana had increased dramatically within a short time.

Just twenty days after it began, Operation Intercept was ended. The precise reasons for its curtailment have not been revealed, but a combination of the following factors may have brought about the decision to call it off: (1) the urging of the Mexican government; (2) the small quantities of drugs seized; and (3) pressures from businessmen on both sides of the border. The full impact of Operation Intercept may never be known. On the positive side it may have deterred smugglers from even trying to bring marijuana across the border. While there were no large seizures of marijuana, there were reports of diminished supplies in some cities. On the negative side there appear to have been several unintended consequences (Gooberman, 1974):

1. Legitimate businesses in the thirty border cities were hurt by as much as 50 percent. Further, many Mexicans had permits that allowed them to live in Mexico but work in the United States and for these people absenteeism was common because of the difficulty in going through the checkpoints.

2. Smugglers learned the advantages of bringing shipments across the border by plane. Although the government had set up sophisticated radar, pilots could simply fly low through the mountains separating Mexico and Texas and avoid it. Many flights were made at night by moonlight.

3. In many cities marijuana was as freely available as before, but where shortages were noted, users often switched to other drugs, often LSD or other hallucinogens. The greatest

increase of all, however, was in the importation of hashish from North Africa.

4. Some of the shortages of Mexican marijuana were made up for by increased shipments of marijuana from other countries, such as Vietnam. Thus the operation broadened the base from which marijuana could be obtained and guaranteed a more stable market in the future.

5. The marijuana shortage (or rumors of it) induced many in the United States to begin growing their own marijuana. One immediate response was to locate and harvest marijuana that was growing wild in many states.

Paraquat

In 1975 the U.S. government entered into an agreement with Mexico to spray the herbicide paraquat on fields of Mexican marijuana, a cheap low-potency variety that constituted most of the marijuana smuggled into the United States. The program received a great deal of attention and did wipe out substantial portions of the Mexican crop. However, what marijuana survived was still shipped north, where it caused widespread concern among marijuana smokers and public-health officials (Falco, 1983).

One immediate impact of this program was to shift to Jamaican and Colombian marijuana, both of which were much more potent than Mexican. Colombia is still an important source of marijuana, jockeying with Mexico for a place as the single largest source for American consumption. In 1984, for example, Colombia was estimated to have provided approximately 48 percent of the marijuana consumed in the United States, compared with only 24 percent from Mexico (NNICC, 1985–1986). In 1985 Mexico came back as the number-one producer (about 40 percent), and by 1989 Mexico was supplying 79 percent of the marijuana used in the United States (NNICC, 1989). This suggests that the long-term impact of these eradication programs may have been slight. "Despite aerial spraying, it has been estimated that about 1,300 tons of Mexican marijuana was available for distribution in the United States in 1983, compared to 750 tons in 1982" (Brecher, 1986:20). Further, these programs had to operate in the face of widespread government corruption. For example, some DEA officials were told that some Mexican eradication pilots had substituted water for the herbicides they were supposed to spray (Anderson, 1985).

A second impact of the paraquat program was to increase domestic production. As one author has put it (Brecher, 1986):

The spraying of foreign marijuana fields with paraquat and other herbicides meant a bonanza for California growers, for U.S. marijuana smokers who had long preferred imported marijuana now demanded domestic marijuana to avoid the adverse effects of herbicide residues. Thus, the foreign herbicide spraying program became in effect a kind of farm-aid program, helping U.S. marijuana growers capture a larger share of the market. (21–22)

Thus, the shift to domestic marijuana may have been due less to limited foreign supplies than to health concerns. Brecher (1986) has argued that while domestic production first started in California, it quickly spread throughout the United States as a result of a spraying program in California modeled after that in Mexico.

The Vietnam War

In his associations with marijuana growers in California, Chapple (1984) attributed the start of marijuana growing in California to the return of Vietnam soldiers who used marijuana and brought back seeds to the United States. These soldiers also brought back a sophisticated knowledge of weapons, booby traps, and jungle warfare, all of which they would use in their marijuana growing.

While there are undoubtedly some cases that fit this profile, there is little evidence that such circumstances were the typical avenue by which growers first began in California—and the scenario may be even less common in other states. (One could just as easily argue that draft resisters were more likely to be growers.) It is more likely that Vietnam was important to the domestic marijuana industry because (1) the war opened channels for transporting Asian marijuana into the United States, making the drug more widely available and, in turn, feeding demand; and (2) if smoking marijuana was a symbol of rebellion against the "establishment" that supported the war, growing marijuana was nothing short of a revolutionary statement.

Paraquat, Operation Intercept, and the Vietnam war set the stage for the rise of domestic marijuana cultivation. In the 1980s this emerging industry continued to expand, partly because of government policies and partly because of the increased popularity of cocaine.

Ironically, the tough government stance against marijuana *imports* in the 1980s may have provided a substantial boost to domestic marijuana farmers. Kleiman has argued that the unintended benefits to domestic growers from this crackdown was "the only successful piece of agricultural policy of the Reagan years" (Johnson, 1989). The domestic marijuana industry in the 1980s was also aided by the increased popularity of cocaine, which led many smugglers to switch from marijuana, the latter being less lucrative, more bulky, and harder to store for long periods without decay. While foreign supplies were constricting, the demand for marijuana remained high. Rising prices and frequent shortages provided strong incentives for people to enter the domestic marijuana business.

SUMMARY

The domestic marijuana industry began in the 1970s and expanded during the 1980s. By 1988 domestic marijuana accounted for as much as a quarter of the U.S. marijuana market, and suggestions that marijuana had become America's largest cash crop were credible, even by the most conservative production estimates. Domestic marijuana not only increased in quantity, but in quality. It is often more potent than imported marijuana and is the marijuana of choice in some regions of the country. The domestic industry also has dispersed throughout the United States. By the mid-1980s, marijuana growers were found in every state, and the number of commercial growers may have been as high as 250,000.

Despite the large impact of domestic marijuana on the U.S. market and the large number of people involved, little is known about those who grow marijuana for profit. Anecdotal accounts, combined with interviews conducted for this study, suggest that while commercial growers are drawn from a variety of social groups, they can be categorized according to their motivations for entering the business. One objective of this study is to more fully describe commercial growers. In the following chapter the focus shifts to a brief description of marijuana botany and the characteristics of the plant which shape the nature of the domestic industry.

5

MARIJUANA BOTANY
AND CULTIVATION

The domestic marijuana industry is shaped, not only by the demands of users and the restrictions imposed by law, but by the nature of the plant and the process of growing. This is a key distinction between marijuana growers and smugglers or street-level dealers. The botany of the plant imposes requirements of time, space, and location on those interested in growing marijuana for profit. In addition, knowledge about the plant aids growers in avoiding detection, while simultaneously increasing potency and yield (i.e., profits). This knowledge is also used by law enforcement to locate growing operations and to determine their sophistication.

Marijuana was given its scientific name, *cannabis sativa*, which is Latin for "cultivated hemp," in 1753 by Carl Linnaeus, a Swedish naturalist and classifier (Merlin, 1972; Grinspoon, 1977). Out of respect for Linnaeus it is sometimes called *cannabis sativa L.* There are disagreements about the classification of the plant, but all marijuana appears to be part of a single species. Within this species are a number of varieties, and both the physical appearance and intoxicating properties vary from one variety to the next. For example, what is commonly referred to as *cannabis sativa* is generally tall (from five to eighteen feet) and is sparsely branched. Its leaves are long, narrow, and light green. Another variety is *cannabis indica*, which tacks on the country of origin (Goldman, 1979). Indica tends to be smaller (four feet or less) and is more densely branched. Indica leaves are a very dark blue-green, sometimes with a purple tinge, and are shorter and wider than are sativas' (Frank & Rosenthal, 1978; Frank, 1989). Indica plants also tend to mature earlier than sativas. Sativa and indica are the two major varieties of marijuana currently cultivated in the United States, and it is common for cultivated plants to have a mix of genes from both varieties.

    Some suggest there are two additional varieties familiar to growers in the United States—*cannabis ruderalis* and hemp (Schultes et al., 1974; Frank, 1988). Ruderalis is a relatively obscure variety of marijuana that originated in Russia and is of very low potency. Ruderalis has few branches, grows to only several feet tall, and matures before either sativa or indica (Frank & Rosenthal, 1978; Frank, 1989)—desirable characteristics for outdoor growers who wish to avoid detection and for indoor growers who have limited space. However, its low potency is a problem for growers and some believe that introducing ruderalis to the U.S. hemp gene pool will eventually diminish the potency of all domestic marijuana (Selgnij & Clarke, 1988).

    Hemp, also called ditchweed, is the term used to describe wild cannabis sativa, which was originally grown for fiber. At one time there was a large hemp industry in the United States, particularly during World War II when sources of sisal rope had been cut off by the Japanese invasion of the Philippines (Solomon, 1966). Today much of this hemp still grows wild, particularly in the Midwest (see chapter 2) where it is known as ditchweed. The large volume of ditchweed still growing wild in the United States is reflected in 1990 figures for the Domestic Cannabis Eradication/Suppression Program, in which 7.3 million cultivated plants were destroyed but over 118 million ditchweed plants were eradicated (DEA, 1990).

    Hemp plants tend to be tall (six to twelve feet) and spindly and are among the heartiest varieties of marijuana. It is said that the seeds of wild marijuana plants have been known to lie on top of the ground for as long as seven years before germinating (Furnas & Bartle, 1988). As an intoxicant, however, wild marijuana is of such low potency that even law-enforcement officers record its destruction under the separate title of "ditchweed."

    Ditchweed is generally a nuisance for law enforcement and commercial growers alike. Law enforcement officials use valuable time supervising the eradication of plants that are of little use to commercial growers but that may be harvested by young kids. Occasionally ditchweed will be harvested for sale or used to "cut" more potent marijuana. This is rare, though, since the penalties are the same for harvesting wild and cultivated marijuana, while the returns from wild marijuana are relatively small. Professional growers find wild marijuana a nuisance because it may contaminate their carefully developed seed stock, or prevent them from growing sinsemilla (see below). Although low in potency, domestic hemp does have the advantage of maturing early and is sometimes crossed with more potent varieties to yield a hearty, potent, and early maturing plant (Frank, 1988).

    Marijuana is easy to breed. Consequently, more advanced growers frequently experiment with crossing varieties to emphasize desired characteristics. These include, not only the manipulation of the plant's physical characteristics (such as height and speed of maturation), but the intensity and nature of the high. The plant prefers open areas and warm weather and needs very little water except during germination and the establishment of its main root. It can grow in a variety of temperature and moisture conditions but grows best in areas with hot summers. Interestingly, the plants that grow around it can influence the hemp's growth. For example, if grown next to spinach or rye, these plants will do very well but the hemp will do poorly. In contrast, the hemp plant does very well if grown next to corn or turnips (Merlin, 1972). Not only do marijuana and corn grow well together, but "marijuana grows best under the same conditions of soil and climate that favor corn: lots of water, especially in the early seedling stage; lots of light; and a soil or loam that is high in nitrogen and potash, moderate in phosphorous and containing little or no clay" (Goldman, 1979:34). Thus, the climate and soil conditions that make some midwestern states large corn producers are also the conditions that make them well-suited for growing marijuana.

For domestic growers the three most important considerations when choosing a variety are yield, speed of maturation, and potency. Each of these factors differs from one variety to the next, and growers continuously strive to develop plants that provide heavy yield, mature quickly, and are very potent.

THC IN MARIJUANA

The active ingredient by which the potency of marijuana is measured is tetrahydrocannabinol (THC). There are more than two hundred varieties of marijuana plant and the concentration of THC differs among them. The potency of marijuana is primarily determined by the variety, although potency can be somewhat influenced by the methods used for growing, harvesting, and storing. THC is relatively unstable and when exposed to air and sunlight breaks down into nonpsychoactive substances. One study found that within a year a sample of marijuana exposed to light and air lost over half of its THC (Fairburn, Liebman, & Rowan, 1976). Exposure to direct sunlight further speeds this breakdown. This is why seeds from Mexican marijuana that has been field-dried in the hot sun may produce domestic marijuana that is *more* potent than the processed marijuana from Mexico. Genetically, the two crops are the same, but the sun-dried marijuana is less potent because the sun has broken down some of the THC.

In addition to THC, the marijuana plant has over 400 ingredients (Wallach, 1989). While the level of THC determines the *intensity* of the high from marijuana, the particular combinations of these other substances determine the *nature* of the marijuana high. For example, the high from cannabis sativa is sometimes characterized as "cerebral, spacey, and energizing," whereas the high from indica is described as "debilitating, stupefying" (Frank, 1988:167,171). Through careful plant breeding, marijuana growers often seek to develop a set of effects in the same way that winemakers breed grapes to produce a particular flavor or bouquet in wine.

Importantly, the potency of marijuana can be increased through plant breeding. "With modern plant-breeding technology, it should be possible to produce strains of grass that are more potent than anything hitherto known and to make the common weedlike strains that grow wild over the Midwest into powerfully hallucinogenic drugs" (Goldman, 1979:34).

The potency of marijuana in the United States has, in fact, increased dramatically since 1970. Some suggest the more potent marijuana of the 1980s is a fundamentally different drug than that of the 1960s and 1970s. They argue that claims of marijuana's relative safety are based on tests with the older, less potent product and that the "new" marijuana poses new risks (Inaba, 1987; Inciardi & McBride, 1989). While marijuana in the 1980s is more potent by as much as a factor of five, it is unclear whether this hurts or helps the health of the typical smoker. Users may become more intoxicated with the new marijuana, making them less safe drivers, for example. It is also true, however, that less smoke is inhaled to reach intoxication, which would clearly be a health benefit from more potent marijuana. However this question resolves itself, Mikuriya and Aldrich (1988) convincingly argue that highly potent marijuana has a long history of recreational use and that calling it a "new drug" is misleading. They also suggest that although new marijuana may be more potent per pound the practice of autotitration, or the self-regulation of doses, means that users are not necessarily becoming more intoxicated. This, too, is an issue that merits further study.

THE SEX OF MARIJUANA PLANTS

Marijuana plants are dioecious. That is, each plant matures as either a male or female, although on rare occasions plants grow with characteristics of both sexes or reverse sex during growth (Frank & Rosenthal, 1978). Plants with the traits of both sexes are known by growers as hermaphrodites. Male plants usually grow somewhat taller and both plants secrete resins that can be used as hashish. Resin does not flow through the plant but is produced by resin glands, which cover all parts of the plant except for the roots and seeds (Frank, 1988). Resin slows water loss in hot and dry environments, and the amount of resin produced is directly related to the climate. Generally, the hotter and drier the climate, the more resin will be produced (Merlin, 1972). The female plants, which produce the most resin, slow down resin production once they are fertilized. People who grow hemp for its intoxicating effects often separate male and female plants before pollination occurs, thus encouraging the female plant to continue producing flowers and hence more resin (see the discussion of sinsemilla below). It is not true, as some believe, that female marijuana plants yield more potent leaves. Actually, the leaves are similar in their concentration of THC, but the female buds are substantially more potent and have considerably more weight (Brecher, 1972).

SINSEMILLA

One of the most potent forms of marijuana is sinsemilla (Spanish for "without seeds"), which is produced by harvesting the resinous buds from female plants. Sinsemilla is *not* a distinct variety or strain of marijuana but is the result of a particular method of cultivation. During flowering, the buds of female plants become sticky with resin (which is loaded with THC). If the flowering female plants are not pollinated, these tops continue to produce both flowers and resin, becoming increasingly potent. Cultivators of sinsemilla kill the male plants as soon as they are old enough to determine the plants' sex—between two and three months after germination. From the remaining female plants most growers harvest only these female bud tops, also known as colas. Although themselves potent, the remaining leaves and stems are generally destroyed because their bulk, relative to their selling price, is much greater, and hence the risk of arrest is higher for a smaller payback. In addition, growers often take great pride in the quality of these flowering tops and, by comparison, see the leaves and stems as inferior products.

Domestic marijuana is increasingly grown as sinsemilla rather than in less potent forms. In 1990 the DEA reported that 28 percent of all eradicated domestic plants were sinsemilla. In 1983 fewer than 1 million sinsemilla plants were eradicated in the United States; by 1988 this figure had jumped to almost 3 million plants, dropping to 2 million in 1990 (DEA, 1988, 1990).

In 1989 the THC content of sinsemilla averaged about 7 percent. This is double the concentration of THC in "commercial-grade" marijuana, which contains some buds (NNICC, 1985–86; 1989), and is substantially higher than the 3 percent THC reported in standard marijuana (DEA, 1988). Potency has also increased over time from an average .5 percent THC level in 1974 (Mikuriya and Aldrich, 1988). According to the NNICC, the highest concentration of THC reported to date was found in a 1986 sample of marijuana, which contained 18.3 percent THC (NNICC, 1988).

As potency increases, so do the profits for growers. In 1989 commercial-grade marijuana was selling for $300 to $2,000 a pound at the wholesale level, while sinsemilla was selling for $700 to $3,000 a pound at the wholesale level (NNICC, 1989). In contrast, ditchweed was selling for only about $50 a pound.

Not only is the type of high shaped by the variety used, but so is the quantity of saleable marijuana per plant. Cannabis sativa, for example, can be expected to yield from one-third to five pounds of sinsemilla buds per plant, whereas cannabis indica generally yields from one-quarter to two pounds per plant. Ruderalis will generally yield between one-quarter ounce and two ounces of sinsemilla buds per plant (Frank, 1989).

THE GROWING CYCLE

Commercial marijuana growing is directly tied to the growing cycle of the plant. Marijuana is an annual plant that is ready for harvest in four to nine months, although there are a few varieties that can be harvested in ninety days. Seeds germinate within four to seven days, and for the next four to six weeks the plant develops leaves and roots in what is termed the seedling stage. The vegetative growth period follows, and it is during this time that the plant grows most rapidly, sometimes as much as six inches per day. It is also during this stage that plants can be sexed and male plants eliminated.

The vegetative growth stage ends between three and five months after germination. The rate of growth slows considerably after this and the plant is soon ready for flowering—an essential development for sinsemilla cultivators. The speed at which the plant matures (i.e., flowers) depends partly on the strain. However, the trigger for flowering is the photoperiod—the length of daylight versus darkness. When the plant is exposed to at least two weeks of more than thirteen hours of continuous darkness each night, it begins to flower and produce the accompanying resin, which covers the buds. It is claimed that by manipulating the photoperiod, plants can be induced to flower within sixty days of germination (Clarke, 1981). Consequently, to the extent that growers can control the photoperiod, they can manipulate the timing of harvest (Frank & Rosenthal, 1978; Frank, 1988).

ATTRITION

Those with little knowledge about growing might assume that the careful grower who starts with 100 seeds will eventually harvest 100 plants. In reality, the attrition (plant loss) during the growing cycle can be substantial. Although attrition varies across growers, batches of seeds, seasons, and geographic regions, a typical grower can expect roughly the following from his 100 seeds. Approximately ninety of them will sprout. Of these ninety, he can expect to lose as many as a quarter to animals, fungus, or plant disease. Of the remaining seventy plants, approximately one-half will be males and must be killed, though some claim that if proper steps are followed during germination only about thirty percent will be males. Of the thirty-five female plants that remain, approximately thirty will grow to maturity and be harvested. This rough accounting of the attrition problem does not include losses from theft, a common problem in some parts of the country. It also does not include losses from grower error, such as overwatering. It does, however, illustrate an important point. When police find a growing operation, the reported number of plants seized may depend on the point in the growing cycle when the seizure is made, whether the grower is cultivating sinsemilla or commercial-grade marijuana, and the extent to which the grower has the expertise or will to prevent losses from disease and animals. Official estimates based on seizures early in the growing season will seriously exaggerate the size of the crop that would have eventually gone to consumers. This discrepancy is an issue when official data is used in states such as Illinois, where criminal charges can be based on the number of plants, regardless of their stage of development. Further, since the effects of climate, disease, and animals are only partially under the control of the grower, early in the season growers themselves can probably report only an approximation of their final harvest.

INDOOR GROWING

During the 1980s, indoor growing became increasingly popular. The DEA reports a steady increase in the number of greenhouses seized, from 649 in 1984 to over two-and-one-half times that (1,669) in 1990 (DEA, 1990). The shift to indoor growing was probably inevitable but, like the domestic industry itself, was probably given a boost by law-enforcement policies. Growing indoors makes police detection less likely by undercutting the usefulness of fly-overs and almost eliminating cases in which innocent citizens stumble upon crops in the wild. Once detected, however, it is generally far easier for the police to tie indoor crops to particular individuals.

Apart from law-enforcement pressure on outdoor growers, indoor operations have probably become popular because they offer the grower almost total control over the growing environment. The indoor grower can regulate temperature, nutrition, carbon dioxide levels, and humidity—all factors that shape marijuana's potency. Perhaps most importantly, indoor growing provides total control over the photoperiod and hence over the speed at which the plants form buds. Indoor operations not only afford increased protection from the police but from animals and marijuana thieves as well. Finally, growing indoors allows for a year-round growing season so that a relatively small space can produce many more plants than the same space outdoors.

While growing a few plants under fluorescent grow-lights from a local hardware store is probably a common practice for small-time hobbyists, it is inefficient for commercial growers. Commercial indoor growers need a host of special equipment and can require an initial investment of up to $5,000 or much more for very large operations. Lights are generally metal halide or high-pressure sodium lamps, similar to those found in some warehouses and street-lights. The grower will also require a device to move the light fixtures around the growing area and thus ensure even lighting. In addition, the grower may require systems for injecting carbon dioxide into the air, timers, fans and blowers, thermostats, humidistats, reflectants, and perhaps even devices to help control the odor (some varieties have a very strong smell while growing). Finally, some growers choose to use hydroponics rather than dirt, rockwool, or some other growing medium. Hydroponics requires additional special equipment.

Thus, commercial indoor growing involves a level of commitment and technical expertise not required of outdoor operations. Some growers compromise by using indoor operations to start plants. The plants are moved outdoors when the weather is warm enough or when the plants are mature enough to be sexed. This also protects seedlings from some kinds of animals and insects. Still more efficient are growers who start plants indoors using cuttings from a "mother plant." This technique not only produces plants with known intoxicating properties but also assures the grower only female plants (except for the few that will change sex during maturation). The process of growing plants from cuttings is sometimes referred to by growers as cloning.

SUMMARY

Marijuana is a hearty plant that can be grown in a range of soil and climate conditions, and the process can be as simple or complex as the grower wishes. There are many varieties of marijuana, which differ in potency, appearance, and the speed at which they mature. Marijuana's potency is primarily determined by the strain used, although it is tempered by the techniques of growing and harvesting. The basic technology for growing is so simple that novices can enter the industry with little trouble, but there are also opportunities for increasing their sophistication and technical expertise. As a rule, the greater the expertise and effort expended, the greater the financial return per plant.

Currently, one of the most potent forms of marijuana is sinsemilla, in which resin-covered flowering buds from female plants are harvested. Sinsemilla's share of the domestic crop appears to be increasing each year. Another trend is toward indoor cultivation, which makes detection more difficult and allows for year-round crops. Space limitations and the cost of utilities also encourage indoor growers to cultivate sinsemilla rather than commercial-grade marijuana.

The fact that the plant is hearty and can be bred to accommodate a variety of growing conditions does not bode well for those wishing to completely eradicate it. Millions of wild hemp plants are eradicated each year, yet they continue to flourish. This is a testament to the problem facing eradicators. Technical fixes, such as spraying poison on plants, may reduce the domestic marijuana crop. However, growing will never be stopped using technical fixes alone. Growers are simply too inventive and the plant too adaptable.

6

THE RESEARCH SETTING

Although much of this study was conducted in Illinois, interviews were held with thirteen officials from five other states, and well over a dozen people familiar with growing in other states. The study is intended to generate information that is broadly applicable while recognizing that social, political, and geographical features of Illinois may also make marijuana growers there unique. During the course of the study, it became increasingly clear that substantial regional variations existed in the nature and extent of marijuana growing and that a national picture of the issue is incomplete without taking these variations into account. Variations among a few select states are addressed in chapter 9. The purpose of this chapter is to describe the setting in which marijuana growing occurs in Illinois.

THE GEOGRAPHY OF GROWING IN ILLINOIS

In terms of land mass, Illinois is the twenty-fourth largest state, and it ranks fifth in population. The state extends approximately 385 miles from north to south and is 200 miles across at its widest point. Except for some hills in the south and in the extreme northwest, the terrain is flat and "differences in elevation have no significant influence on the climate" (*Climates of the States*, 1980:234).

Summers are hot and humid, with temperatures topping 90 degrees for an average of twenty days in the north and fifty days in the south. Although there are sometimes droughts, as in the summer of 1988, these are rare and usually isolated. April-through-September rainfall ranges from twenty-one to twenty-four inches throughout the state, with the most rain falling in May and

June.   In general, the elaborate irrigation systems that are essential for
marijuana growers in northern California are less critical in Illinois.

The average date of the last spring freeze generally ranges from April
5 in the south to May 5 in the north. The average day for the first freeze of
fall ranges from October 5 in the north to October 25 in the south (*Climates
of the States*, 1980).   Thus, even in the cooler northern half of the state,
marijuana growers can expect an outdoor growing season of at least five
months.

Overall, the soil and climate are excellent for agriculture, and
consequently for marijuana growing. Illinois is among the leading states in the
production of corn and soybeans. The soil tends to be the richest in the central
and north-central portions of the state and it is in these regions where
agriculture is most profitable.

The southern part of Illinois is less suited to agriculture. The terrain
is more hilly, there are more forested areas, and the soil is poorer. While the
average rainfall is greater in the south than in the north, most of this excess
occurs during winter and does more harm than good by eroding the soil and
leaching out minerals from the soil (*Climates of the States*, 1980). During the
Depression, many farms in southern Illinois went bankrupt and the government's buyout program resulted in the creation of the Shawnee National Forest,
which covers 256,000 acres. Because of the way in which it was created, the
Shawnee National Forest still has many pockets of private land that provide
unobtrusive access to isolated areas of the forest, a fact that has not been lost
on marijuana growers.

THE SOCIAL SETTING

Much of the state is rural, with approximately half of the population
concentrated in Cook County (Chicago). Compared with southern counties, the
northern half of the state is economically prosperous. In addition to agriculture, a crisscross of rail lines, and later interstate highways made the central
and northern regions of the state well suited for the development of a broad
economic base. Today it is in the south, where local economies are weaker and
unemployment is higher, that cultivated marijuana is more commonly grown.
It is also the southern part of the state that has a history of resisting government regulation of private activities. Moonshining, for example, was a common
practice in southern Illinois during prohibition.

Southern Illinois has a history of poverty, racial hatred, and lawlessness
that distinguishes it from the northern portion of the state. At one time coal
mining was a major industry in the area. Violent strikes were relatively
common and the area gained a reputation for lynchings and mob justice. Over
time mining became more mechanized and the industry no longer required a

large labor force. In the absence of alternative industries, unemployment has often been high.

Historically, Williamson County is the most notorious of southern Illinois counties and the area is sometimes referred to as "Little Egypt." Several historians have commented on the unique social features of this region. Littlewood (1969), for example, has observed:

> From its earliest days Egypt acquired a reputation for bloody violence and disregard for law and order. Many of its people were prejudiced, stubborn, and hot-blooded. Social control was deemed a family function. Law enjoyed no particular prestige value. . . . One plausible theory for the regional history of violence is the fact that the region was peopled before it was governed. There were no courts, sheriffs, or constables, so the people learned to solve their problems themselves by direct action rather than through the recognized channels of organized society. (74)

In his study of this county from the 1870s to the 1920s, historian Paul Angle (1980) notes:

> Williamson County, Illinois, I believe, offers an almost unrivaled setting for a study of this phenomenon [violence]. There one can identify a wide variety of causes—family hatreds, labor strife, religious bigotry, nativistic narrowness, a desire for money and to hell with the rules. . . . With the possible exception of Harlan County, Kentucky, I know of no other American locality possessed of these attributes. (ix-x)

Of course, lynchings and mob violence are no longer features of southern Illinois life. In fact, during the 1980s the index crime rate was lower in the southern part of the state than in the north. Nevertheless, the past does shape the contemporary culture of the area. A strong suspicion of government authorities is still more characteristic of southern Illinois than of the rest of the state, and it is in this region that marijuana growing seems most entrenched. It is probably no accident that this southern region of Illinois also shares borders (and many social values) with Missouri and Kentucky, two states that the DEA lists among the top five for marijuana production in 1990 (DEA, 1990). To the east is Indiana, which is routinely among the top states for the eradication of wild marijuana, or ditchweed, and which ranked twelfth in the eradication of cultivated plants in 1990.

During the course of this study, two small projects, funded by Illinois State University, were designed to describe the social climate under which marijuana laws are enforced in Illinois. In the first study, conducted in the

summer of 1989, random digit dialing was used to survey 100 Illinois households outside of Cook County regarding the use of the law to regulate
marijuana. The second study examined the same issue using a mail survey of
Illinois criminal justice officials. Conducted during the fall of 1989, this survey
included responses from 217 judges, 244 police chiefs, 87 sheriffs, and 74 state's
attorneys (Weisheit & Johnson, in press).

These surveys found that both citizens and criminal justice officials
across the state believed there was widespread public support for enforcing
marijuana laws. Although both groups thought few marijuana users were
arrested and that even unlimited police resources would not stop the problem,
there was strong support for using tough criminal penalties against those
involved with marijuana. Among public officials, there was nearly universal
agreement (95 percent) that politicians in their jurisdiction would hurt their
chances of election if they supported reductions in the penalties for marijuana
offenses. Similarly, most felt there would be public support for the full
enforcement of marijuana laws, that is, always arrest and give maximum
penalties.

These survey findings were generally confirmed in interviews with
growers and law-enforcement officials. Most citizens in Illinois are neither
supportive of marijuana growing nor critical of aggressive police efforts to curb
growing. The hostility that some nongrowing citizens have reportedly shown
toward marijuana eradicators in northern California and parts of Kentucky has
not been seen in Illinois.

MARIJUANA ERADICATION IN ILLINOIS

Nearly all marijuana eradication in Illinois is conducted by either local
sheriffs or the Illinois State Police (ISP). The ISP, through its Cash Crop
Program, is responsible for conducting investigations, making arrests, and
storing and coordinating information about marijuana cultivation from
throughout the state. In some counties, because of a shortage of manpower or
as a matter of personal preference, sheriffs have routinely turned over all leads
regarding cultivation cases to the ISP. In others, local sheriffs take the lead in
cultivation cases, calling in the ISP only when the case is very large or where
complicated issues of forfeiture may be involved. Through the 1980s the trend
has been for an increased role for the ISP, although there are still a few
counties where cultivated marijuana is defined as a purely local problem.

The Cash Crop Program was begun by the ISP in 1983 with support
from the federal government, which was helping other states institute similar
programs. In the beginning the Cash Crop Program was operational only
during the fall harvest season. By the late 1980s, the rise of indoor growing and
an increased appreciation for the extent of the problem resulted in the year-
round operation of the program.

Nationally, the State of Illinois is not one of the top states for the eradication of domestic marijuana. The 1987 DEA cannabis eradication report ranked Illinois as twenty-fifth in the number of plants eradicated and in 1988 the state's ranking had dropped to thirty-second. Since then, the seizure of several large fields has caused the state's ranking to rise to fifteenth in 1989 and eighth in 1990. Whatever the specific ranking of the state, it is fair to say that Illinois has been and continues to be an average or typical state in regard to the amount of domestic marijuana eradicated.

The ISP has generously shared summary data from the Cash Crop Program spanning the years 1983–1989, although the most complete data exist for the years 1987–1989, when most of the records had been computerized and when information was broken into a larger number of categories. These data allow for a description of broad patterns and trends in growing marijuana in Illinois, keeping in mind the limitations of using official records to make such generalizations.

Between 1987 and 1989, the ISP Cash Crop Program contained records on 524 cases in which either cultivated or wild marijuana plants were eradicated. Cases were reported in ninety-one of the state's 102 counties, with seventy-four counties reporting cases of cultivated plants and forty-seven counties reporting cases of wild marijuana. Of the twenty-eight counties reporting *no cases* of cultivated marijuana, twenty-two were in the north or north-central regions of the state. The 394 cases of cultivated marijuana involved 98,012 plants, and 112 of these cases resulted in an arrest. Thus, the arrest rate *for identified plots only*, is about 28 percent. The number of cultivated plants per case ranged from none (where the plants were removed before the police arrived) to over 58,000, but in most cases the numbers were relatively small. The median number of plants per case was only eighteen, below the cutoff used for inclusion in this study. In fact, only 192 of the 394 cases (49 percent) involved twenty plants or more and of these, fifty-eight resulted in arrest (30 percent).

In addition to cases of cultivated marijuana, there were 130 cases in which wild marijuana was eradicated. These cases involved 301,311 plants and led to seventeen arrests. Unlike cultivated marijuana cases, it makes little sense to talk about arrest rates involving wild marijuana, since it frequently grows without planting and will often not be harvested. Unfortunately, national data on seizures and arrests combine cultivated and wild marijuana. Nationally, about one in ten eradicated plots results in an arrest (see chapter 4). In Illinois, arrests in cases where either cultivated or wild marijuana plots are discovered occur about 25 percent of the time.

There were variations by region. Figure 6.1 graphically illustrates the distribution of cultivated marijuana plots eradicated in Illinois and Figure 6.2 illustrates the distribution of wild marijuana plants eradicated, based on police records. Only 20 percent (77 of 394) of cases involving cultivated marijuana

Figure 6.1
Cultivated Marijuana Plots Eradicated by County, 1987–1989

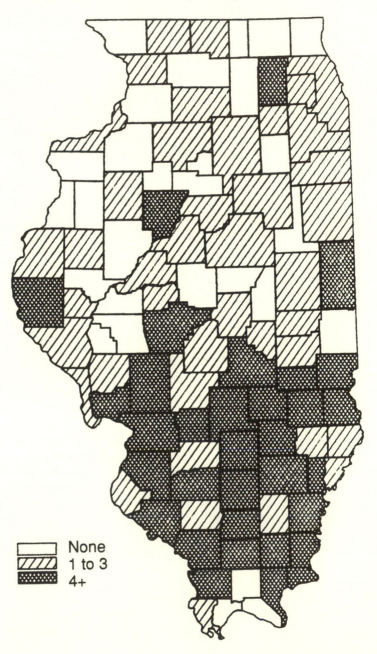

None
1 to 3
4+

Figure 6.2
Wild Marijuana Plots Eradicated by County, 1987–1989

None

1 Or more

were in the northern half of the state. In contrast, northern counties accounted for 84 percent (109 of 130) of wild marijuana cases. In general, those counties that account for most of the eradication of cultivated marijuana are not those in which wild marijuana grows most freely. One can only speculate, but historical and economic factors may provide a reasonable explanation for this pattern. During World War II hemp was grown in the northern part of the state, which has the richest farmland. Because the marijuana plant is very hearty, hemp first planted during World War II continues to flourish despite years of eradication efforts.

It is sometimes argued that eradicating wild marijuana is important because (1) it provides young people with a low-cost entry point to the use of marijuana, and (2) wild marijuana somehow gives people the idea to grow or provides them with enough knowledge of the plant to enable them to cultivate more potent varieties. The first point is beyond the scope of this study, but interview data from police and growers raise questions about the extent to which this is a problem. If anything, the low potency and foul taste of wild marijuana may deter new users from experimenting further. The second point is called into question by the fact that counties with large amounts of wild marijuana are not those with the greatest problems with cultivated marijuana. This second point is also given no support by the interview data. In fact, for the serious marijuana cultivator, wild marijuana is likely to be more of a curse than a blessing, as discussed in the next chapter. The professional grower of sinsemilla who is "shopping" for a place to grow marijuana is likely to avoid those counties where wild marijuana is most abundant.

SOCIAL AND ECONOMIC CORRELATES

A detailed analysis of the link between social and economic factors and the epidemiology of marijuana growing in Illinois is beyond the scope of this study. It is possible, however, to briefly address this issue by combining county-level data on marijuana seizures with county-level census data on employment and family income. Table 6.1 shows the association between the number of cultivated plots eradicated and several social and economic factors.

Table 6.1 is striking for the consistent lack of association between marijuana seizures and poverty-level and unemployment rate. These economic factors are poor predictors of counties in which marijuana will be cultivated. The lack of association between seizures and population density also undermines arguments that marijuana growing is largely a function of the isolation of remote rural areas. In itself, remoteness cannot explain why cultivation is more common in some counties.

Table 6.1

Correlation Between Marijuana Eradication in Illinois Counties in 1987–1989 and Selected Social and Economic Factors

Variable*	Cultivated Plots	Wild Plants
Population Density	n.s.	n.s.
Percent Below Poverty Level	n.s.	n.s.
Unemployment Rate	n.s.	n.s.
Crime Rate	n.s.	n.s.
Percent Minority	n.s.	n.s.
Region**	.29	-.24

Sources: Illinois State Police; U.S. Census.

N = 102 Counties

*n.s. = not significant; all other correlations are significant at the .05 level

**1 = North; 2 = North-central; 3 = South-central; 4 = South

As the next chapter shows, commercial marijuana growing in Illinois is restricted to members of the white majority. Table 6.1 suggests that the lack of minority participation in Illinois is not exclusively a function of small minority populations in rural areas. In fact, two of the southernmost rural counties in Illinois are nearly one-third minority citizens.

The table does show the predicted association between marijuana growing and region of the state (the only significant associations in the table). The southernmost counties are those most likely to report cases of cultivated marijuana while the northernmost counties are those most likely to report cases of wild marijuana.

These patterns of association are particularly interesting when examined further. Density, poverty, unemployment, and minority population are not related to marijuana seizures, while region is associated with seizures and sighting wild marijuana. At the same time, region *is* significantly correlated with density, poverty, unemployment, minority population, and crime rate. It is particularly interesting that the southern portion of the state, where cultivated marijuana is more often detected, has a lower index crime rate than does the northern half of the state.

It is clear that whatever impact economic factors have is not direct. These economic and social factors may interact with other cultural features of these regions to shape the production of marijuana. Further study of these patterns may be useful in explaining patterns of marijuana growing in other states as well.

SUMMARY

This study was conducted in Illinois, an average state in regard to the eradication of marijuana, but a state with enough climatic, geographic, social, and economic variability to provide a good setting for studying a range of people who grow marijuana for profit.

Although the soil is richer in the northern half of Illinois, marijuana growing appears more frequent in the south. This is apparently the product of both cultural and economic factors, although a precise understanding of the role of these factors was beyond the scope of this study. No direct association was found between county-level marijuana seizures and unemployment or poverty, but these factors are related to region of the state.

While there may be regional variations in marijuana growing, there seems to be a general consensus by citizens and criminal justice officials that laws against marijuana growing should be rigorously enforced. There appear to be few (perhaps no) pockets of organized community support for marijuana growers in Illinois, as has been seen in Kentucky and California.

7

WHO GROWS AND WHY

A major objective of this study is to provide descriptive information about domestic marijuana growers. This is done using public records and interview data from the thirty-one domestic growers, thirty-three officials familiar with domestic marijuana cultivation, and over a dozen people with some knowledge of marijuana cultivation. (Details of data collection procedures for each group are presented more fully in Appendix A.) Input from officials is discussed in chapter 9. This chapter focuses on growers, utilizing public records and their own statements.

GENERAL CHARACTERISTICS

Understanding commercial marijuana growers begins with a brief description of their social characteristics. This profile includes age, sex, race, occupation, mobility, education, and prior contacts with the law.

The growers in this study ranged from 25 through 66 years old at the time of their arrest, with a median age of 38 years. Many are of the Vietnam era, although only three had served in Vietnam and none of these three cited experiences there as shaping their decision to grow marijuana; nor did their experiences in Vietnam provide them with technical knowledge of marijuana cultivation. One grower did, however, obtain his seeds from Afghanistan through a friend in the military.

As might be expected, most marijuana growers were male. In only two cases were females the primary growers, although there were several cases in which females played secondary roles. In both cases with females as the primary growers, the operations were well below average in size and complexity, and in both cases the growers were relative neophytes.

Just over half of the growers were married at the time of their arrest. In these cases wives were sometimes used as partners or helpers in the growing operation. It sometimes happened that males would grow without the knowledge of their spouses, to shelter them from legal punishment. As a methodological note, growers who worked with their wives in the growing operation were less likely to agree to be interviewed than were those who were either unmarried or whose wives had no role in the operation.

Perhaps the most striking and consistent finding was that only one case involved a minority grower, and this individual argued he was not growing but was the victim of tenants who had been growing on his land. The absence of minority growers was not only true in our group of interviewed offenders but was true for every case we had located.

The lack of minority involvement in commercial marijuana growing may be partly due to the rural setting in which growing takes place. While the State of Illinois is 17.3 percent minority, the two top counties for marijuana seizures were .4 percent and 1.8 percent minority, respectively. Further, none of the top five marijuana-cultivating counties in Illinois had a percentage of minority citizens greater than one-half the statewide average.

Although the rural setting undoubtedly contributes to the lack of minority involvement in marijuana growing, that is not a sufficient explanation. As was seen in the previous chapter, there is no correlation between the amount of marijuana eradicated in a county and the percentage of that county's population which is minority. There are minorities in rural communities, and as will be seen below, there is nothing special about obtaining the materials or knowledge for growing that would preclude minority participation. In short, there is no obvious explanation for the lack of minority involvement in marijuana growing in Illinois.

The lack of minority participation also appears to hold outside of Illinois. During the course of an interview for this project, the author of a well-known how-to book on marijuana growing confirmed this pattern in his observations in California, New York, and elsewhere. Since he became involved with marijuana in the 1960s, he could recall only one minority grower.

In his study of marijuana arrest data in California, Mandel (1988) argues that the increasing proportion of minorities arrested for marijuana cultivation and dealing during the 1980s could have been the result of increased enforcement that drove white marijuana growers from the business, leaving a vacuum that was filled by blacks and hispanics. This was speculation on his part, however, since his data did not allow him to separate possession and dealing from cultivation. Although enforcement against cultivation did increase during the 1980s in Illinois, there is no evidence that minorities were moving in to fill positions left by white growers.

The lack of minority involvement further illustrates the point that the association between income and growing is complex. While marijuana growing overrepresents white citizens in Illinois, the average income of caucasians is higher than that of minorities.

At the time of their arrest, only four of the thirty-one interviewed growers were unemployed. Of the remaining twenty-seven growers, nine were farmers and the rest held a variety of jobs, often running their own small businesses. These included such occupations as auto mechanic, tavern owner, photographer, carpenter, and masonry worker. As a group, these growers were employed but had limited incomes, a fact that many attributed to their decision to begin growing. Those working for someone else commonly lost their jobs when they were arrested.

Stereotypes often depict those in the drug business as unemployed and making luxurious incomes from their drug activities. Neither was true for this group, but recent research suggests that these stereotypes are also untrue for urban street dealers, who often have legitimate employment and choose to supplement their legal income with a modest income from drug sales (Reuter, MacCoun, & Murphy, 1990).

Most of those arrested were long-term residents of their local communities. At the time of their arrest only three had lived in the community for less than seven years and over half had lived there all their lives. Consequently, most local residents personally knew either the grower or members of the grower's family.

These growers were not only stable employed residents of the community in which they were arrested, they were also relatively well educated. Only three of the thirty-one had less than a high school education.

In seventeen of the thirty-one cases there were also prior experiences with the criminal justice system, although only six had prior arrests related to drugs. Only two growers had previously spent any time in prison.

The most serious prior offense was committed by one individual who had previously been arrested for assault and battery. Other arrests were for disorderly conduct, drunk driving, and reckless driving, often when they were quite young. For several growers prior records were exclusively for minor crimes, including "driving before he had his license," "trespassing by fishing in a power ditch," and "possession of a stolen bicycle frame." With a few exceptions, these growers could not be characterized as members of a "dangerous criminal class." While most had a rough familiarity with legal procedures, several were strikingly naive. In one case a judge asked the grower if he had an attorney, to which the grower replied, "Why do I need an attorney, your honor, I'm guilty."

To summarize, these growers were white, middle-aged males with long-standing ties to their communities. Nearly all were employed at the time of their arrest, most having been either farmers or self-employed. Those who worked for someone else commonly found they were fired as a result of the arrest. Just over half had prior arrests, but these were usually for minor offenses, and for the most part they had relatively short offense histories. The focus now shifts to the process by which these individuals entered the business of growing marijuana, and gained the necessary technical knowledge about growing.

CHARACTERISTICS OF THE OPERATIONS

In presenting a backdrop for interpreting the interviews, it is important to give an overview, not only of the growers themselves, but of their growing operations as well. As noted in an earlier chapter, arguments that arrested growers will include only those most naive or least skilled at avoiding detection are undercut by the finding that growers in this study had been involved in the business for an average of five years, with one grower having been involved for eighteen years. Aside from one case in which the individual primarily harvested wild marijuana, most of these cases involved the labor-intensive cultivation of high-potency sinsemilla. In addition, most of the operations were outdoor (25 of 31), although several of the indoor operations were extremely sophisticated.

Not only were these growers experienced, but the typical operation was rather large. By the growers' own accounts, the largest operation had over 6,000 plants, with a median of seventy-five plants. As an interesting method-ological note, official reports placed the median number of plants at 193, well over double the number reported by growers. Part of this discrepancy is probably due to the tendency for growers to minimize what they were doing and for officials to exaggerate it. More important, however, is the difference between growers and officials in the way they count plants. The discrepancy between grower and police accounts is likely to be particularly large when the plants are seized early in the season and are very small. Officials usually count every plant they find, including those recently germinated. Growers, however, think of plants more in terms of how many will likely reach maturity and therefore exclude diseased plants or "volunteers" that are to be weeded out (see chapter 5 on attrition). This is one reason why, at the time of the arrest, police were often able to give a far more precise count of plants than were growers.

Finally, there is the issue of income from marijuana growing. Many growers were uncomfortable talking about their illicit income. Most of their concern was that the Internal Revenue Service or the police would somehow use this information against them (despite a promise of confidentiality). Thus, those who made the most from marijuana growing were least willing to provide much specific information about their income, although a few very large operations must have been very lucrative.

Other growers had difficulty specifying the cash income from their operation, either because they were just getting started and had yet to realize any income or because the income varied so much from year to year. These fluctuations were the result of variations in weather, problems with pests, theft, seeds that would not germinate, and so on.

Whatever their situation, the growers in this study expected to receive between $700 and $1,500 a pound for their crops. Several were willing to accept the smaller amount in exchange for having the buyer do the harvesting and/or manicuring, that is, trimming leaves from the buds and discarding much of the stem and leaves. A few had made plans for freezing a portion of their harvest for later sale. In this way they not only had a more regular source of income from the marijuana but could sell it months later when domestic marijuana was in short supply. During these periods they anticipated receiving as much as $2,000 a pound for their crop. While there have been accounts of marijuana selling for as much as $3,000 a pound, growers in this study did not receive that much.

In terms of net profits, these growers represent the full range. A few barely broke even, if they counted the cost of their labor. At the other extreme were cases in which the grower became quite wealthy. Most cases probably fall somewhere between these two extremes, although it is impossible to be more precise than that.

GETTING INTO THE BUSINESS

To understand the process by which people enter commercial marijuana growing and their approach to their illegal activities, it is helpful to utilize the typology of growers outlined in chapter 4. During the course of the study, it became clear that the typology fit these cases well and provided a useful framework for analysis. To briefly summarize, the three types of commercial growers are:

1.   *Hustlers*, who take on marijuana growing because it is a business challenge. They are motivated less by the money itself than by the success it symbolizes. Because they view their enterprises in grandiose terms, small growing operations are of little interest to them. Numerically, this type is probably the most rare, but because of the scale of their operations, they may contribute significantly to the illicit marijuana market.

     Locating hustlers is particularly difficult because, like large entrepreneurs in the legitimate business world, they are not always involved in the day-to-day work of the operation. This provides them both social distance and legal safety from the operation they run. In contemporary political jargon, they provide themselves with "deniability" for any involvement with marijuana growing while simultaneously being in a position to profit from their activity. Hustlers are also likely to commission those in financial trouble (i.e., pragmatists), who provide the labor and sometimes the land. In exchange, the hustler provides seeds and markets the crop.

2. *Communal growers* who become involved in the marijuana business as part of a larger lifestyle, in which marijuana plays a part. Nearly all begin as marijuana users and take up growing for their own consumption. Economic necessity or peer pressure may push them to grower larger crops. If these economic problems pass, they are likely to continue growing, although they may scale back their operation. This group by far constitutes the major category of growers in this study.

3. *Pragmatists* who enter the marijuana business out of economic necessity. They may or may not be users of marijuana. They would rather not be in the marijuana business but feel there are few options available to relieve their economic problems. Unlike the hustler, they are in the marijuana business to help them through tough economic times, not to become wealthy.

In the discussion that follows, most illustrations are drawn from interviews with either communal growers or pragmatists. This is not to downplay the significance of hustlers. Although the number of hustlers may be small, their operations tend to be quite large, and large operations contribute substantially to the domestic marijuana market. For example, between 1987 and 1989 in Illinois, of the 394 cases of cultivated marijuana recorded by the Illinois State Police, only 10 (2.5 percent) involved more than 1,000 plants. Yet these 10 large cases accounted for 80,056 of the 98,012 plants eradicated during this period, or 82 percent. Even excluding the exceptional case of 58,000 plants, the remaining 9 cases accounted for 55 percent of the eradicated plants. Similarly, cases involving 100 or more plants accounted for 15 percent of the cases but 92 percent of the plants. Compared with other types of growers, hustlers are fewer in number, less visible, and are probably less likely to agree to be interviewed.

GETTING STARTED

There are several avenues by which people who decide to grow marijuana get started. Those who do not themselves use marijuana or who have little interest in it may be taught about it and provided seeds by acquaintances who are into the marijuana culture. The relative number of growers who begin this way is very small and these growers are nearly always pragmatists.

The most common avenue for entering the marijuana business is for marijuana users to begin with seeds they find in the marijuana they purchase. They often begin growing marijuana out of curiosity, viewing it as an amusement or hobby that saves them the expense of purchasing marijuana from others. If they are successful in their early efforts, they may try to improve their product by obtaining seeds from better strains:

Q: When you first started growing, where did you get the seed? Was it from the stuff you were using?

G21:   Right, right. When I first started growing, it was from commercial street pot. Just your average marijuana you can buy off a dealer. I used them for a year and a half, so I knew the end product was directly linked to the variety of the seed. So, I was in search for better seed. I knew somebody who had a brother in Dwight and occasionally sent him, through the mail, little amounts of pot. I acquired some seeds from him. I started growing them for about a year and it was quite a bit better. But then I learned of some seed banks in The Netherlands and sent for them. . . . I was leery at first. I didn't know if they were legitimate businesses or not. I didn't know if they were a rip-off or not. But, I took a chance, sent for some catalogs, got them back, and finally placed an order. I received my seed right through the mail. When I grew that, I could tell right away that was the way to go. When it harvested, the first batch, it was just unbelievable how good it was.

Growing marijuana for profit requires not only access to seeds but to a market. Because of their sensitive nature, questions about markets avoided details that might incriminate others and focused instead on the general structure of the distribution chain. Because of the structure of the distribution chain, this area of questioning did not prove very fruitful. The smallest growers generally sold only to a small group of friends, no more than twelve to fifteen people, and often fewer. As the size of the operation increased, the number of people to whom the product was sold diminished. The very largest operations sold only to one or two buyers, and growers seldom had any idea of where the marijuana went from there. In fact, many did not want to know what happened to the product after it left their hands, since this information was of no practical value and might work against them in the event of arrest.

As discussed later, many of these growers felt it very important that young people not have access to marijuana. By selling only to trusted friends, small operators could control this aspect to a large extent. Large operators, by not knowing the destination of their product, could mentally separate their growing activities from marijuana use by young people. This provided large growers with yet another reason to remain uninformed about what happened to their crop after it left their hands.

Whatever the avenue by which these growers sold their product, none of them indicated experiencing periods in which there was no demand for it. To the contrary, many reported there were chronic shortages of high-quality marijuana. One even indicated that an acquaintance who had been buying small amounts for years sometimes required two months to find high quality marijuana. Although this pattern was confirmed by police, it seems to contradict high school surveys in which students report marijuana generally available throughout the 1980s (Johnston, O'Malley, & Bachman, 1988). One explanation for this seeming contradiction is that the United States has two marijuana markets. One caters to less-discriminating buyers, such as high school students, and includes marijuana of highly variable quality. In this market shortages are infrequent. A second market caters to highly selective users who demand (and recognize) high-quality marijuana and are willing to pay high prices. Shortages in this market are more frequent because the marijuana itself is more labor-intensive to produce and is less amenable to mass production. This study was not designed to examine marijuana markets, but the existence of two distinct markets is consistent with available evidence.

LEARNING ABOUT GROWING

Part of the appeal of marijuana growing, aside from the potential profits, derives from the characteristics of the plant itself. It is a hearty plant that nearly anyone can grow. Unlike creating synthetic drugs, almost no knowledge is required to begin growing marijuana. To the contrary, states in which marijuana was planted for hemp during World War II have found it almost impossible to eradicate (see chapter 2). At the same time, it lends itself well to more sophisticated breeding techniques and growing technologies. Thus, even as a hobby, it can be as simple or as complicated as the grower wishes.

Consequently, there are two distinct levels of learning. The first and simplest level requires only the skills necessary to sprout seeds and grow plants to maturity. A basic knowledge of gardening is usually sufficient. By using seeds of highly potent varieties, a beginner can grow marijuana profitably with only this basic level of knowledge. When growers were asked where they first learned how to grow marijuana, several seemed surprised that the question was even asked:

G08:   I'm a farmer. That's all you need.

G07:   I just learned by trial and error. I mean, I grew up on a farm,
       so I know about growing corn and soybeans. It wasn't much
       different.

G16:   Well, I'm a farmer for one thing, and I just learned from
       growing all those years. See I progressed through the years,
       I learned how to do it.
Q: You didn't use any books?
G16:   I did after a while when I started to grow. It helped a little
       bit, but mostly I just learned on my own.

G18:   It's easy. Easy if you know the right people. And, even if you
       don't, like I said, if you want to grow dynamite pot, just grow
       it like you would a tomato plant. There's no problem. It'll
       shoot right up there.

G30:   Sure, anybody can do it. I mean, you just have to have a
       handful of seeds and some halfway decent soil. . . . if you can
       put a seed in the ground and grow a garden, you can grow
       marijuana.

G28:   Well, some of my friends were farmers, and you know, this is
       a farming community. A lot of people you know are from the
       farm. I've been out working and helping on farms. So, it
       would be pretty hard not to learn about farming, unless you
       just stuck your nose in a book without learning something.
       Too many people talk about it, so you just pick up a little
       here and there. And then, I like to garden. . . . and I did a
       lot of reading and studying about how to make a better
       tomato or just anything. Any problem there was, I wanted to
       figure out how to get around it.

Q: How much did your knowledge of farming help you in trying
       to grow marijuana?
G24:   It helped a great deal. But I don't think you have to be a
       farmer to grow marijuana. Knowing about commercial
       fertilizers and herbicides and things like that was helpful.

Nearly all of the growers said that when they began there were people
they knew who could answer questions they had about growing. Although the
advice was often given within the context of marijuana, general information
about growing plants was usually all that was needed. A few purchased
magazines and books, but for this level of growing sophistication such materials
were not essential. These materials did reassure growers that they were doing

the right thing, and for those with no knowledge of plants, they were a substantial improvement over trial and error. It is possible that such materials improved the success of novitiates who otherwise would have become frustrated and quit. However, none of the growers in this study reported that books were a deciding factor in their continued growing.

On the whole, books and magazines about growing marijuana probably have little impact on the growing of simple cultivated marijuana outdoors. The process is so straightforward that books are generally unnecessary. Interested growers can get all the information they need from friends, trial and error, or from experience with growing other plants. One grower said that when he had doubts about fertilizer or bugs he simply went to the local garden shop and framed questions as if he were growing tomatoes.

Growers arrested in their first year were more likely to be discouraged and frustrated with growing. They were least experienced with growing marijuana and consequently had the most problems in growing. In addition their expectations were often unrealistically high. Rather than emphasizing the ease with which plants grew, they expressed frustration:

G26:   I didn't really have much of a chance to get going. I didn't
         really have any great success or anything. Some of them were
         a little bit bigger than others. I liked them better because
         they grew a little faster. I don't know if I really reached a
         point where anything from this experience was very satisfying.
         As a matter of fact it was a big disappointment.

Unless they could overcome these initial frustrations, these individuals were unlikely to have the commitment to become long-term growers. Consequently, any study that focuses on people who have been in the business for several years must keep in mind this process of self-selection.

A second level of knowledge about marijuana growing requires more technical sophistication. It is the knowledge required to do plant breeding, cloning, indoor growing, and hydroponics. Here again information specific to marijuana is useful, but for many growers general information from books on botany and horticulture served just as well. Several growers said that organic gardening books and magazines were particularly useful:

Q: Growing itself is no big problem?
G18:   No. It's pretty much easy. I had some in-depth studies in an
         encyclopedia about diseases of plants—a whole encyclopedia
         for plant growing.
Q: Oh, really.

G18:   Also there was the magazine, *Organic Gardening*. They provided me with a lot of inside information. They never knew it, but that's what they were doing.

Q: Did you have any books specifically for marijuana?

G18:   Oh, yeah.

G10:   I got most of my information on how to grow pot from reading. Like, I subscribe to *Organic Gardening*. But, I started buying *High Times* magazine, and they have articles in there all the time about how to grow pot. And I even sent away for a videotape on how to grow pot.

In fact, a leading developer of hybrid marijuana strains in Holland, who was interviewed in *High Times* magazine, claimed to have simply applied to marijuana the principles he learned when breeding parakeets as a young man. An illustration of how even the most general growing information can be applied to marijuana, which was also the most unusual source of technical information reported in this study, was one grower's account of how he learned about the process of grafting:

G18:   I even spliced some [plants] together, you know, took a plant, cut this stalk off, sliced it in there, and so on. They showed it on Mr. Roger's show. I thought "Well, they can do that, let me try it here."

Q: That's a source I hadn't heard of before.

G18:   Well, he was doing a show one day and I was sitting with the kids. All of a sudden here he is slicing a plant and taping it back together. Okay! So I went down, took the Colombo plant and put some sinsemilla on it.

Two of the growers in this study had become informal technical experts on growing, providing advice to friends on a range of topics, including plant diseases, cloning, and breeding. They actively experimented with various growing techniques and took a great deal of pride in being able to show others how to improve the quality and yield of their crops. This was not undertaken as a moneymaking activity; their services were often provided at no charge.

Q: Did you have people you could turn to if you had questions?

G21:   No, because I kind of led the field with this. I was the first one in our area that I knew about that started this. And I gradually told more and more people, and the people that I had told turned around and told people. They were always turning to me because I pretty much knew more than them because I just took it upon myself to gather as much knowledge about it as I could. I had quite a bit of literature on it. I had books, magazines, and so forth that I always read through and they were turning to me when they had problems. There were a number of times that I would go over to their house and try to analyze the problems they were having. Many times I helped them out. Eventually though, when they got on their feet, they didn't need my help anymore. It's pretty easy once you get the hang of it.

Q: Wasn't it risky telling other people that you were doing this?

G21:   It was a closely knit group of friends, close friends that I work with or that I have known practically all my life. I didn't see any risk or threat involved. It never turned out that way.

Such sources as *High Times* magazine or *The Marijuana Grower's Guide* were commonly used by advanced growers, and most of these growers had one or two trusted friends who also grew and with whom they exchanged information. Published materials on marijuana growing appear to have an important role in teaching about more sophisticated growing techniques, such as cloning, crossbreeding, and producing sinsemilla. They may be particularly relevant for indoor growing where they provide information about regulating carbon dioxide levels in the air, as well as humidity and temperature, and modifying the length of "days" under artificial light. These techniques, however, are not those of the first-time grower but are utilized by those who already have a basic knowledge of growing and usually some fascination with the growing process. As illustrated above, experienced growers were also likely to utilize general books and magazines on organic gardening and horticulture.

Recently, some local jurisdictions have considered banning instructional materials on growing marijuana by defining them as paraphernalia. Such a ban would probably serve as a mild deterrent to beginners who have no one to serve as a mentor. It might also reduce the number of growers who graduate from simple to more sophisticated techniques. The problem, however, is that marijuana growing can be profitable even if only simple techniques are used. Banning these materials will not stop domestic marijuana production, but it probably would have an impact on the utilization of the most sophisticated techniques. Banning these materials may also be of some symbolic value. These books do give the interested reader the sense that growing marijuana is not only easy but socially acceptable and widely practiced.

PROBLEMS IN GROWING

Mastering the basics of marijuana growing is relatively straightforward. Even people with little gardening experience seldom require more than a growing season or two in which to acquire the basics. This is not to suggest, however, that after the seeds have germinated the grower can merely sit back and relax until harvest. Several growers commented on the amount of work involved. This was particularly true if the growing involved sinsemilla outdoors and in a large plot or group of plots.

Q: Was it a lot of work taking care of the plants?

G28:   Yes, a lot of work, to do it right.

Q: Someone described it as a weedy garden.

G28:   Well, especially in the early part [of the season] it is. Near the end it isn't. Do you know anything about putting out corn?

Q: A little.

G28:   Once it gets past knee high, you know, it kind of shades itself out, and pretty much takes care of the weeds; and marijuana was something like that. The problem is up through June or July it's pretty bad. You're working quite a bit, keeping the weeds down, fertilizing it. Then you fight fungus sometimes, or at least we did. I don't know about other people.

G24:   Being a farmer, the biggest part is getting the seeds. Marijuana is a lot like any other plant. You fertilize it. It's a broadleaf, so you use grass weed killer on it just like you do your soybeans. A little manual labor and away you go. I don't want to make it sound too simple. It's not really that simple. It takes a lot of work. . . . It's a labor-intensive crop. I suppose it's similar to tobacco.

Q: You did all the harvesting and grooming yourself?

G29:   Yeah. That takes time. It's a lot more work than most people think it is.

Q: Some people said they were thinking about getting out because it is hard work.

G29:   Yeah, it is. I mean you've got to go out there and take care of your plants at night—late in the evening you get bit up with mosquitoes and ticks. There's a lot of work. I tell you what. If they legalize it, a lot of people might just grow enough for their own use, but they won't grow for money—unless they've got machinery. They're not going to do a lot of work.

G02:   The idea about income from growing is overblown, it's all
         overblown. People think you grow a plant and you make a
         million bucks. That's ridiculous. . . . once you get it done and
         you look at all the work, the months it took, the whole idea of
         setting everything up to make it work, getting rid of your
         crops—you've done a lot of fucking work for a little bit of
         money. And if you'd had a good job at $10 an hour or
         something like that, this whole fucking mess would have been
         a waste of time.

        In his discussion of the rise of the cocaine industry in South America,
Bagley (1988) compares the labor involved in marijuana and cocaine production:

         Marijuana is essentially a labor-intensive process; the employ-
         ment and income multiplier effects are therefore more widely
         distributed. Cocaine requires fewer people, more capital and
         at least an incipient industrial process relying on imported
         chemicals. It demands financial skills to handle the much
         larger profits which are heavily concentrated in a few hands.
         (76)

        Aside from the work, there were three areas in which growers faced
problems. There were pests, thieves, and the police. Pests were a general
nuisance which, with a little effort, could be controlled. Thieves and the police
were less predictable and controllable and were the source of considerable
anxiety for some growers.

        Most growers experienced problems with pests, which included mice,
grasshoppers, deer, and rabbits. The particular pest and the extent of the
problem varied from one case to the next, although problems usually occurred
when the plants were young and tender. As the plants matured, few animals
would bother them. What was interesting about these pests was the way in
which growers responded. Despite the potentially high costs these pests might
incur, responses were relatively nonviolent. Insects, of course, could be
controlled with insecticides, although this itself posed some hazard to the
consumers:

G19:   I had grasshoppers one year so bad they stripped the plants.
         I went out there one day and there was nothing but stalks, just
         like beetles do your beans [soybeans]. So next year we
         sprayed them with chemicals. Then when stuff was real dry
         and tight [hard to get] we took the leaves, dried them and
         then we'd smoke 'em. Man, you'd get some hellatious
         headaches. I mean some hellatious headaches. . . . So we
         found out that before you smoked it, you washed them down

and let them get some natural rains and then there were no problems.

To drive away small animals, such as mice and rabbits, growers purchased repellent that could be applied directly to the plant or placed around it. Others used techniques that were quite creative.

Q: Did you have trouble with animals?
G07:   Deer would chew it off. They only do that when it was small, deer and rabbits, mostly deer. But after it got past ten or eleven inches high, it would be pretty safe. I finally worked that out. I would just take a couple of buckets of dog shit out there, and scatter it around. That would keep the deer off.

Q: Did you have any problems with rabbits or deer?
G18:   I've never had any real problems. Human urine is the best prevention, I think. If you are going to plant some, you might as well step away from them ten feet and take a leak. That's probably the most effective thing you can find. . . . I knew a guy who used mothballs, but I've never tried that.

G18:   Deer and rabbits [were a problem]. The only thing you have to do is, if you have a plant here, put a salt block over there. The deer will go there and won't even mess with the hemp. For rabbits all you have to do is take chicken wire and go so high up around the plant, and you haven't got a worry in the world.

Many of the techniques were analogous to folk remedies, with growers firmly committed to their approach and scoffing at the folk remedies of others. For the most part, pests were merely a technical problem which, with some trial and error, could be brought under control. More difficult were problems with thieves and police.

G09:   It probably took a couple of years before I really got the click of it, where I probably saved 90 percent of what I set out [from pests].
Q: That's a pretty high percent.
G09:   Yeah. Of course, you really can't do it anymore. I mean, anymore you don't worry about the police, you worry about thieves. The police are no problem, it's the thieves. I mean, everybody's out looking around for other grower's patches.
Q: You did have people steal your crops?

G09:   Oh, yeah. I don't know, I figure maybe 20 percent of what
         you put out you're going to lose to thieves. Maybe 5 percent,
         to cops bothering you, or maybe more like 2 percent.

Q: You had it growing in your garden?
G07:   Yeah. See, I used to grow it out along the river banks, but
         people ripped it off all the time. I got pretty proficient at it
         and I had some pretty good stuff, and people would know it.
         They would look for my truck. They'd see my truck out
         someplace three or four times in a row and they'd know that
         down there someplace, I'd have some reefer growing. Just
         local people, you know, and they'd go out and rip it off.
Q: You had trouble with people stealing your crops?
G07:   Yeah, and it was always people who knew me, cause they'd
         know my truck and they knew that I grew reefer and that I
         did a pretty good job. So they'd see my truck four or five
         times or more in one place, especially if it wasn't a good place
         to be fishin', cause I fish a lot, too. If they knew it wasn't a
         good place to be fishin', they'd know what was going on out
         there, and they'd go out and rip it off.

Q: Did you have any trouble with people stealing your crop?
G14:   Yeah, that's a big deal anymore, too, you know. Instead of
         messing with doing it themselves, like I said it's a lot of work,
         a lot of people just go out and hunt it. Especially in the fall
         of the year, it's still green, cause it'll stay green clear till
         Christmas if you leave it out there.

Q: What were you doing at the time of your arrest?
G16:   I was out in the field. I had it all cut down and I was burning
         it. They [the police] saw flames or smoke shooting up so they
         came hurrying back there to catch it before it all burned up.
Q: So, you knew the police were on the way?
G16:   No. I was just burning it because somebody ripped some off.
         They took the best of it. Instead of letting them have the rest,
         I just decided to burn it.

For some growers, problems from thieves or the police were taken as
simply the risk of doing business. They knew they were taking a gamble but
calculated that the odds were in their favor. For others, however, concerns
about thieves and the police generated considerable anxiety.

Q: Is it stressful growing marijuana?

G09:   I would go for days without sleep. So many things turn your head, mainly stress. Of course, I talked to a lot of people, you hate it, but yet you love it. Like a lot of people go to war I guess. Well, basically it is is war. You hate it but you love it. I guess it's the adrenalin, the excitement in a boring life. But yet there are limitations to excitement.

Q: While you were growing, did you feel tense or nervous?
G22:   Oh, yeah. It's just the fact that it's getting close to the time that you are going to have to harvest and you're not sure if somebody is watching you. You just get real paranoid.

G28:   It [the stress] built up. Well, even after the first year of harvesting stuff, it was nerve-racking. It got to be where going down the street—maybe I'm going ten or fifteen blocks away—by the time I get there I might have been going forty or fifty. If somebody started to follow me, or was just behind me and I didn't recognize them and they went for more than three or four blocks, I'd make a left or right turn or some-thing. Paranoid, I guess you'd say. I don't know how many times I went in and ordered a beer or a cup of coffee or a meal and left most of it. You know, how some people will look over at people, and maybe I felt they looked too many times, and I'd just get up and leave.

Each of these problems, including the anxiety, was magnified for outdoor growers where the plants were exposed to pests, thieves, discovery by passersby, and the police. This provided an incentive for some to begin growing indoors.

Q: So, you always grew indoors?
G21:   Yes. I've dittled around outside a little bit, but it's pretty hard to grow outside. It's hard to find location, and when you do find location, it's pretty isolated. You need a lot more time to tend to them. And there are just too many pests. If they do make it through the summer, towards the fall, then you have to worry about thieves coming out there and whether or not there's anybody hiding out in the woods. Too many negative factors involved that make it worthless.

Most growers in this study raised marijuana outdoors. Only fourteen of the seventy-four cases identified for this study (and six of the thirty-one interviewed) involved indoor-only operations, although several had started plants indoors to get a jump on the growing season and to sex the plants before putting them outdoors. This reduced their risk of detection and saved them from the problems of starting plants outdoors.

THE REWARDS OF GROWING[1]

In chapter 4, the cash value of marijuana was discussed, and many journalistic accounts focus on economics as the sole motivating factor for commercial marijuana growing. The emphasis on cash rewards has character-ized much of the writing about the drug trade in general, beginning with a 1969 article by Preble and Casey in which they described the life of an addict as "a career that is exacting, challenging, adventurous, and rewarding" (2). By the 1980s studies were examining street-level drug organizations in which the sellers were not addicts, often were not allowed to use drugs while working, had a strong commitment to the work ethic, and viewed their activities as a career (Mieczkowski, 1986; Williams, 1989; Fields, 1986). Increasingly, drug dealing has come to be defined within the context of "drugs as work" (Manning & Redlinger, 1983).

While money is important—perhaps the most important reason for commercial marijuana growing—it is not the only factor motivating these growers, and this is particularly true for communal growers. For many of the growers in this study, the intangible rewards of growing seemed to rival cash benefits as motivating factors. There were at least three ways in which those who found the process of growing itself rewarding and satisfying. Growers tended to emphasize either the spiritual, the social, or the intrinsic rewards from growing.

Several spoke of the *spiritual rewards* from growing, using religious or almost-religious descriptions of their feelings. The process of growing, as distinct from the money or the effects of using marijuana, was something they spoke of with great passion.

Q: Aside from the money, was there anything else about growing marijuana that you found satisfying or enjoyable?

G03:   This plant of all the Lord's plants is the most intriguing plant that I know of. Yes, I would grow this plant as some people grow roses. I think roses are dumb even though I grow them and like them. Bananas are a lovable plant and so is papaya, but marijuana is in a category all by itself. I would class it as one of the more sophisticated plants. Yes, I took great pride in producing a high-quality product for my fellow man to enjoy. I have brought much happiness and well-being into this world. To me this is one of the miracles of this world that the Lord has given us such a worthy plant for us to enjoy.

G02:   There is something about growing a marijuana plant, unless
         you do it you don't understand it, because it is a beautiful
         experience. I'm talking from a spiritual sense in that you
         nurture, you work, you learn, and then you—I tell you, I used
         to go out late at night, and lay down under my plants and
         watch the moon pass through those beautiful buds and just
         smoke one and lay there and watch the moon pass through
         them, just amazed. You know there are moments in that
         period that I just, I loved, I just loved it.

It is ironic, perhaps, that in several ancient civilizations marijuana was
treated as a mystical plant provided by the gods (Chopra, 1969; Abel, 1980).
Similarly, the contemporary hemp movement seems to grant such mystical
qualities to the plant, seeing it as a solution to a variety of problems, from
global warming to faltering rural economies. Perhaps the most explicit
statement of this position is Jack Herer's book *The Emperor Wears No Clothes*
(1990), which is subtitled "The Authoritative Historical Record of the Cannabis
Plant, Hemp Production, and How Marijuana Can Still Save the World."
        More common than a concern with spiritual issues was an emphasis on
the *social rewards* from growing. Many enjoyed impressing their friends with
the quality of their crop, and if they had acquaintances who grew, there was
clearly some friendly competition among the growers. What was important for
them was not the fact of their growing but the quality of the product they grew
and the status from having others recognize a job well done.

G21:   Once I started growing I gave away a lot to close friends that
         was just as good as the commercial stuff that they were paying
         for on the street. I just gave that stuff away.
Q: Did you have a lot of pride in that?
G21:   Yeah, I did. So many people couldn't believe the potency of
         it and if you had any sense of pride and accomplishment you
         felt it. . . . Me and my girlfriend did a really good job mani-
         curing the leaves and we took pride in that. A lot of the
         other growers didn't do a very good job at it. But everybody,
         when they looked at the appearance of it, they could tell that
         we had done a good job and they complimented us on that,
         too. So, yeah, we had intense pride. Also we always tried to
         outdo the other growers and we usually succeeded there. It
         was obvious people knew about it from what they said so we
         had a sense of pride about it.

Q: And, you felt a lot of pride in the quality of plants you were
         growing?

G10:   Yeah. In the plants I got caught with in the house. I had
        budded those out in midsummer in the house and we had
        been smoking it all summer. And I was letting other people
        smoke, friends of mine. They said, "Oh, this is the best pot
        we've ever smoked." You know, I had this great feeling of
        accomplishment. When you get done, come out back and
        look at my vegetable garden, and you'll see. I've got radishes
        and onions, and all that, ready all ready. Yeah, well, you see,
        that year I didn't grow any garden, cause I was obsessed with
        growing pot.

        I go out for the awards. I want to be the best. The
        same thing happened to me with the pot. I got obsessed with
        growing it. I wanted to outdo all those guys. I wanted to
        have the best pot, you know. When you grow a garden you
        want to have the biggest tomatoes or whatever. As a hobby-
        ist, you know how hobbyists get involved, so sometimes they
        were obsessed with their hobbies too. Well, that was my
        hobby that year, and I thought at the same time I could have
        enough stashed to last me a year or two. And I even had in
        my mind that I could make some money, cause things were
        financially tough because I went through a bankruptcy.

Q: You felt a lot of pride in the quality of the plants you were
        growing?
G09:   Oh, yeah. You take a big pride, especially when people get
        it, you got better than anything else, than somebody else
        around, I don't know how to put this tactfully, it's kind of, I
        mean, you're not a woman, you can't satisfy someone in that
        way, but there, no matter if they're a whore on the streets,
        some people are going to be, cause they need that relief, that
        satisfaction. You give them a form of relief and they're kind
        of grateful to you for it, even if they are paying a ridiculous
        price for it.
Q: So, aside from the money, you were helping people out?
G09:   Oh, yeah, in a way.
Q: Did you use hydroponics or anything?
G09:   Oh, yeah, I used hydroponics. When I first got into it, I did
        a lot of experiments. I learned how it works. Yeah, it was
        great it was fun, it was a blast. And of course, I wasn't
        worried about getting busted. Then all of your friends get
        into it, you know. It's something everybody starts getting into.
        Something to sit around and talk about. Some people get into
        cars, some people get into plants.

Q: Aside from the money was there anything you really found satisfying or enjoyable about growing?

G04:   Oh, yeah, like I say, I was addicted to it. And I grew really good reefer. I mean it was good quality, very potent. Everybody who tried it, liked it. They always wanted to buy it, and I usually held on to it, and just sold some when I needed the money. You know, when the bills got due, I started falling behind, then I'd sell some to pay the bills. I could have sold tons of it I would guess. Far as I could tell, there was an unlimited demand.

The social rewards from the drug business have been noted by others (Mouledoux, 1972; Goode, 1970). For example, in his study of psychedelic drug dealers, Langer (1977) observed that:

> The desire to obtain profit was played down and those dealers suspected of being interested in drugs for monetary reasons were subject to severe sanctions and ostracized by customers. Generally, the "value" of drugs was as much a social concern as an economic one. (378)

Similarly, Adler's (1985) study of upper-level cocaine dealers recognized the importance of social relations and informal networks that both reinforce and facilitate involvement in the drug business.

Finally, a number of growers reported that growing provided them with *intrinsic rewards*. For these growers the process provided the kind of self-satisfaction that many people find in hobbies with which they become deeply enmeshed.

Q: Aside from the money, was there anything about growing that you found enjoyable or satisfying?

G22:   I was growing a high-quality product. It was kind of rewarding to see all your work turn into something that was going to be nice.

Q: You obviously got more out of it than just saving money.

G21:   Well, I enjoyed doing it a lot. I just took great interest in it. I've always had one main hobby. A long time ago as a teenager it was building model airplanes, small engines like solid engines. Then I went to motorcycling for a while, dirt bikes, then firearms. When I got my fill I had reloading equipment, small arms, handguns. I just had to give all that up. I had $2,500 of reloading equipment alone. My girlfriend used to help me with that. In the meantime we did grow but on a small scale. I had a good job. I made about $15.00 an hour. It didn't bother me to buy pot. But after I saw that film [on growing] I found myself more involved in my pot-growing hobby. It kind of got out of hand. This judge, your know, he wouldn't understand my view on it. Basically it was just an extensive hobby with rewards that I could enjoy. Not only could I save money but I could get high too and I enjoyed doing that. In the long run I'm paying for it now.

Q: Aside from saving money on buying, is there anything else about growing marijuana that you found satisfying or enjoy-able?

G08:   Oh, yeah, I liked to grow it, it's just like growing a nice patch of sweet corn and getting kind of proud of it. Maybe you have a friend come over who enjoys smoking a little marijua-na, and you say "Hey I grew this," and he says "Oh wow, that's nice shit." You know that's just like taking a nice bunch of tomatoes to your grandma's. So, I guess I more or less took pride in a good job, everybody does that, whether it be building a birdhouse, or growing something. Well I like just being a nature person, you know I enjoy it, whether it be pot or some other plant. I just seemed to always be growing things and I'm kind of a green thumb, you know, a horticul-turist I guess. My grandmother had flowers of every variety. I used to help her, so maybe that's where I got the interest. I've got all kinds of house plants, it's just another plant to me.

Q: Was there anything really enjoyable about growing marijuana?
G07:   Oh, sure. Just the same thing that anybody finds enjoyable about having a nice garden, you want to take pride. I always have a good garden, you know, nice tomato plants and pepper plants, and like that. The same that anybody takes in growing anything that they do a good job on.

Q: Aside from the money, was there anything you found really enjoyable or satisfying about growing marijuana?
G09:   Probably the most therapeutic thing I've ever done, just planting it. A lot of people get into planting for the first time in their life and say this is something you've done, you can see for yourself. Of course, then another aspect of marijuana is what it does to the inside of your mind, just what it does to you. The more you get into it, you learn you can control the different varieties of highs or whatever, and it seems like the

more you get into it, the more you learn, the more exciting it is. There's just an initial therapeutic thing being out there, and watching your plants grow. That self-satisfaction does something, even on its own, cause I even got into pot when I was a kid. I mean I didn't smoke it. I didn't know anything about drugs, but it had always grown around there everywhere, it was so thick, and I was kinda interested in it. I tried it a couple of times, the wild stuff, it gave me a headache, and I never could figure out why anyone would pay money for the stuff. But, it had always gotten my curiosity up.

G16:   Well, I enjoy doing it. Yeah. It's just like I grow a big garden. We have a garden out here with sweet corn, all kinds of stuff. I like growing things, always have. We farmed all our lives.

Q: Aside from the money, and saving money from buying, was there anything enjoyable about growing?
G18:   The sweet smell. I'd open that hatch and my whole house would just smell.
Q: You really enjoyed the whole process of just growing stuff.
G18:   Right. Not only pot, I mean, I like plants, too, other plants, house plants. If you leave my yard, it's got a lot of weeds, I don't grow them. But I don't mind growing, I like it. It was a place to get away. I'd be down there four hours maybe inside this great big old sweaty room with a bunch of pot.
Q: Kind of relaxing, huh?
G18:   Yeah, it is calm and relaxing, and the pot plants they like mellow music too. They seem to grow better. You put rock and roll, something loud, harmful, the vibrations, they kind of, I don't know, but if you put on like dentist's music, nice, soft, like Barry Manilow, they like that.
Q: Did you feel any, while you were growing, did you feel any pride in the quality of the plants you were growing?
G18:   I loved them, they were just like kids. I was so sad to see them go. I mean, all this time and dedication. . . .
Q: By "sad to see them go," you mean harvest time and time to cut them you'd hate to. . . .
G18:   Oh, I wouldn't kill them.
Q: You mean killed when they were seized.
G18:   I never, ever killed a plant.
Q: Oh, you just took cuttings off of it?
G18:   You prune them and you shave them. Like cutting your little boy's hair. You always want to save a little piece of it. Haha. You could grow one stalk and let it produce six harvests

off of it. And then once it gets too old, that's when you cut
it down.

Q: Euthanasia, then? Kill the old when they can't go anymore.
G18:   Right. Well, they can, but the quality would start going down.

This same grower even used his operation as an opportunity for
spending "quality time" with his young son:

Q: You did all the harvesting yourself?
G18:   Me and my little boy. He'd be down there with his Tonka
        trucks. I'd say "bring it over here." I'd clear off some buds
        and load them up in his Tonka truck and he'd take it over
        there. We had a lot of fun. He felt bad because they [the
        police] took my plants too. He knew it was pot. I did explain
        to him what it was, and he was mad because the officers took
        my garden.

Intrinsic rewards are not simply the product of putting a seed into the
ground and watching it grow, but of the fact that growers can make their
"hobby" very complex.

G21:   Well, I think it was 1985 when I ordered my first batch of
        seed [through the mail]. And from '85 up until the spring of
        '89 when I got my last batch, I placed four orders. All
        together I had sixteen different varieties. See, they kept
        coming up with new varieties. I was just curious and interest-
        ed in the different varieties they had. They had quite a bit to
        choose from. You can obtain different kinds of high, whether
        its Indica plant, which gives you like a narcotic high, kind of
        a sleepy, heavy high. Or a Sativa plant that gives you a more
        uppity high, kind of a tricky high they call it. Some of it you
        can almost trip on. And in between, there were hybrids. But
        there was more than just the reason of trying to obtain a
        certain type of high. The Indica was the fastest growing, the
        easiest to grow, and the heaviest yielding. But the Sativa grew
        tall and sparse. It didn't yield that much, and it took a long
        time to grow, but it had the best high. So then, you tried to
        find something in between. And that's what I was doing. I
        just kept going around trying to find which would be the best
        to grow, and I was going to narrow it down to two or three
        varieties. That was one of the reasons I had so much at the
        time. I started with about six different varieties for one; you
        have to narrow it down to your best plants. Then you just
        grow them for awhile and make sure its what you want. Then

you can just keep one plant and make that your mother plant, grow it in a separate building and just keep cloning from that, from then on out. That mother plant will last three to five years. Then that way you can grow nothing but females when you clone off the female mother plant. They're nothing but females and they're all pretty much identical. They grow just like the mother plant you take it off of. That's what I was trying to achieve, but I had so many different varieties, I hadn't quite narrowed it down. I tried explaining this to the judge. He couldn't comprehend why I had so much. I was trying to tell him this was the process you had to go through.

PRAGMATISTS VERSUS COMMUNAL GROWERS

Positive experiences with growing were common, but the level of enthusiasm shown in these illustrations should not give the impression that every grower felt this way. Pragmatists, in particular, were more likely to be motivated by little more than money. They were also likely to define cultivation as work, an unpleasant task that had to be done.

Q: Aside from the money, was there anything else about growing marijuana that you enjoyed or found satisfying?

G29:   Ha-ha. No, not really.

Q: Did you feel any pride in the plants or their quality?

G29:   No. I mean, quality I guess, but you know I don't smoke. It didn't do me any good. The only thing I was in it for was the money.

Q: Other than the money, was there anything you liked about growing marijuana?

G01:   No, it was hard work. Well, I guess you could compare it to a weedy garden. It was a real pain in the neck, and I'd go through a 72-tablet container of Rolaids every three days. It just killed me. I hated it, the guilt, you know, of this stuff maybe getting in the hands of kids, or just being illegal. I love this country passionately, and just doin' something under Uncle Sam's nose, I *hated* it. It even had a physical impact on me.

Q: Aside from the money, was there anything else you found enjoyable or interesting about growing?

G30:   Just dollars. Just the money.

Q: Did you feel any pride in the quality of plants you were
        growing?
G30:   Only if it brought money. Only if I could sell it.

        This group, for whom marijuana was nothing more than a source of
income, was very much in the minority. Understanding what motivates most
growers requires appreciation of the rewards from growing that go well beyond
the cash realized by these growers.

HARVESTING WILD MARIJUANA

        Without understanding the pride and satisfaction that some growers
feel from producing a potent product, it is difficult to understand the attitudes
of these growers toward the harvesting of wild marijuana. In general, those
growers who took pride in their product had nothing to do with harvesting or
using wild marijuana, defining that as the province of kids and rank amateurs
in the marijuana business.
        There are only two reasons for harvesting wild marijuana, either for
direct use or for mixing with more potent marijuana to increase the profits of
the seller. Professional growers in this study seldom did either. For them, it
would have been analogous to the maker of an exclusive fine wine selling a
cheap imitation or using cheap wine to dilute his high-quality stock.

G20:   If anybody mentions ditchweed, their noses turn right up, like
        ugh. As if that's like going out and eating dirt. You don't do
        that.
Q: So it's something you'd sell to someone who doesn't know any
        better?
G20:   Yeah.

Q: To your knowledge, does anybody in this area ever harvest the
        wild stuff to mix with other marijuana?
G15:   Over the years I've known different people who have done
        that. Mostly it's kids who run out and harvest it, not to mix
        with anything, just to smoke it and try to sell it to make a few
        dollars. In some cases adults have done that. Nobody I knew
        personally, just somebody that I knew of. Usually they get
        arrested.

Q: Did you ever harvest any of the ditchweed, the wild marijua-
        na?
G21:   Yeah, a long time ago.
Q: For selling or for using?

G21:   Not for selling. Everybody knew what that was. You know,
        ragweed, ditchweed, whatever. When things were real dry,
        when there wasn't any pot for one reason or another, every-
        body got the idea to get some ragweed just to have something
        to smoke. Nine times out of ten it was just a waste of time.
Q: Is that something that is very common, harvesting it?
G21:   Ragweed? No. I'd say that's just something for young
        people, like teenagers, high school kids.
Q: It's not something a professional grower would do?
G21:   No, no, not at all.

Q: You said you didn't harvest any of the wild stuff. As far as
        you know, does that happen very often?
G22:   Oh, it happens some I think. You hear about people coming
        up from St. Louis or down from Chicago, and they see this
        stuff growing. These are people who don't know anything
        about marijuana.
Q: Is this something a professional grower would do?
G22:   No. Because there is no dollar value there.

Many of the southernmost counties had no ditchweed, but where it was
available, it was not only avoided by growers but caused problems for those
cultivating sinsemilla, the unfertilized female hemp plants.

Q: Is the harvesting of ditchweed something a professional
        grower would do?
G18:   No, they won't even fuck with it. If they are any bit of a good
        person, they won't even fuck with it. I mean if they are
        growing for cash they don't care about ditchweed. But when
        I was growing outside, if there is a ditchweed plant even a
        mile away and it comes pollen time, the pollen would carry
        over to your plant. If you've got sinsemilla, a female plant
        with no seed, it will pollinate it. It will trash out yours and
        you'll get all kinds of seeds in it. The stuff will be good but
        it will be full of seeds. You want to get rid of the ditchweeds.
        Just kill them son of a bitches.

The problem for the professional grower is not only that ditchweed
spoils his sinsemilla by introducing seeds, but the seeds are themselves not
usable for later generations of plants because the potent strain of marijuana has
been diluted by the ditchweed. The problem for law enforcement is that
whatever victory is gained by diluting the grower's marijuana stock, the current
crop is still highly potent and future plants that may germinate on their own
may be considerably more potent than the original ditchweed.

Money can be made from harvesting wild marijuana, but the $50 to $100 a pound it yields is small when compared with the $700 to $2,000 a pound from cultivated sinsemilla. Several factors make harvesting wild marijuana a bad deal for professional growers.

First, the legal penalties are the same for wild and cultivated plants, but wild marijuana is far more bulky, increasing the risk of detection. And because it is less lucrative, the seller must deal with a larger pool of buyers to make a comparable income, and this also increases his risk of arrest.

Second, the seller of wild marijuana is forced to deal with less discriminating users, often teenagers. As a group, they are a less dependable outlet, requiring a larger pool of customers. These customers are also less likely to have any personal ties to the harvester. Thus, they present a greater risk of official detection than a smaller group of friends who are seasoned and selective consumers.

Third, harvesting ditchweed often means selling to young people who know little or nothing about marijuana. This is something that many professional growers find abhorrent. Although the professional's crop may be consumed by teenagers, this is not the intended market, and many take elaborate steps to at least rationalize to themselves that kids are not obtaining their product. Such pretexts are almost impossible for the harvesters of ditchweed.

Finally, harvesting wild marijuana offers none of the opportunities for pride in growing skill or for experimenting with growing. The concern with producing a "quality product" makes little sense for marijuana that is so low in potency that the user is more likely to receive a headache than a high. The harvester of ditchweed has no personal stake in his final product.

Professional growers distance themselves personally and professionally from the harvesters of ditchweed. As the preceding quotes show, harvesting wild marijuana is in itself seen by professionals as an indicator of the individual's disregard for quality and his lack of personal standards.

A ditchweed harvester was interviewed during the course of this study. As might have been predicted from the interviews with professionals, he had no knowledge of marijuana cultivation and shared none of their appreciation for subtle differences among varieties of marijuana. He was harvesting and selling ditchweed to support his dependence on other drugs.

It was previously noted that the domestic marijuana market may actually be two markets. One appeals to young, naive, and indiscriminating marijuana users, many of whom have little money. The other marijuana market caters to seasoned, selective users who are somewhat older and have more disposable income. These interviews suggest that running parallel to these two distinct user groups may be two distinct supply mechanisms.

SUMMARY

The typical grower in this study was in his late thirties, white, male, and a long-term community resident. There was only one minority grower among those interviewed, and apparently there were none among the remaining cases we located in Illinois occurring between 1980 and 1990. At the time of the arrest most had been employed. About one-third were farmers. The rest held a variety of jobs, frequently owning small businesses. Although employed, most had modest incomes, and financial problems often provided an incentive to begin growing, or to shift from growing for personal use to commercial growing. Just over half had prior experiences with the criminal justice system, although these were usually for minor offenses and only two had previously spent any time in prison.

The typical grower had been growing for five years at the time of the arrest, with one having been involved in the business for eighteen years. Most had been growing outdoors and were cultivating sinsemilla, the more potent and labor-intensive variety of marijuana. The operations ranged from twenty (the minimum set for inclusion in this study) to over 6,000 plants, with a median of seventy-five plants. Growers could expect to receive between $700 and $2,000 a pound for their product and could plan on harvesting between one-half and one pound from each plant. In practice a few barely broke even and a few appeared to have become quite wealthy. For most it was a modest supplement to their legitimate incomes.

Most were marijuana users and began growing by taking seeds from marijuana they purchased. Those who did not use obtained seeds from friends who used. The purchase of special seed stock generally occurred only after the grower had become proficient at raising and harvesting seeds from commercial marijuana. Learning to grow was straightforward for most growers, particularly those who were farmers and already understood the principles of fertilizing and pest control. Even for those with little prior horticultural experience, learning the basics of growing seldom took more than a season or two. Books and magazines on growing were used as growers became more advanced, though general books on organic gardening were often as useful as those specifically written for marijuana.

Outdoor growers had problems with thieves and pests and often described marijuana as a very labor-intensive crop. Concern with detection by police, losses to thieves, and pests led several to either shift to indoor-only operations or to start plants indoors and then move them outside to finish growing.

Among communal growers in particular, growing was motivated by much more than simple financial gains. These growers realized spiritual, social, and intrinsic rewards from their operations. Spiritual rewards were those feelings of satisfaction expressed in almost transcendental terms. Social rewards included the pride that came from impressing fellow growers and users with a highly potent product or with a product with an unusual form of high. Finally, intrinsic rewards were the feelings of self-satisfaction that arose from the process of growing itself and were comparable to the feelings of many people who become deeply enmeshed in hobbies. The frequency with which growers reported feelings of pride and satisfaction from their operations suggested that understanding what motivates marijuana growers requires an appreciation of these intangible rewards.

Given the pride they show in their products, it is not surprising that most commercial growers looked on the harvesting of wild marijuana (ditchweed) with some contempt. In fact, there are good reasons to believe that professional growers and the harvesters of ditchweed are feeding different marijuana markets. In Illinois those counties in which most ditchweed is eradicated are not those in which most cultivated marijuana has been found.

NOTE

1.   The discussion of rewards from growing draws from materials
      presented in Weisheit (1991a).

8

ISSUES RELATED
TO GROWING

This chapter focuses on a variety of issues related to marijuana growing. These include avoiding detection, violence in the marijuana industry, drug use by marijuana growers, the impact of the arrest, and the community response to the arrest.

The primary defense against theft and arrest is to avoid the detection of the plot by others. Once the plots are discovered, other protective measures may come into play, an issue that is discussed more fully in the next section on violence and the domestic marijuana industry. The issue of avoiding detection was asked of growers in two contexts. First, growers were asked what protective measures they took before their arrest. Second, they were asked what they would do differently if they were to enter the business again, or what growers in general can do to avoid detection.

Prior to their arrest, several growers took minimal precautions or no precautions at all. These growers lived in relatively remote areas where there was little likelihood of their crops being stumbled upon by chance. And, since most had lived in the area for many years, they had a good knowledge of just how accessible their plot was to hunters, hikers, or neighbors.

Q: Did you do anything to reduce your risk of being caught by the police?

G04:   Not too much, really. I wasn't a big-time dealer. I believe I had a reputation for a top-quality product and nobody had any complaints about it. They were all quite pleased to get it. I think you can get into trouble with the police if you try to rip people off.

G06:   I was pretty stupid about doing it actually. I planted stuff
        around it, but it was probably too close to the road, and out
        in too open of an area.

G08:   No, I didn't. I didn't consider it such a crime.

G16:   It was out in a wooded area. Other than that, not really.

G24:   I had mine growing in the center of my farm and there
        weren't any trees close by. So I didn't have to worry about
        squirrel hunters stumbling upon it or anything. It [the field]
        was surrounded by corn. So I really wasn't concerned about
        anybody stumbling upon it. . . . No, [I didn't do anything]
        other than having it in the center of the farm where I thought
        nobody could see it and planting them close together. It only
        got about five feet tall. They were in a soybean field. The
        soybeans were approximately four feet tall. So you couldn't
        really see them unless you went looking for them.
Q: Weren't you concerned about the soybeans turning brown
        while the marijuana plants were still green?
G24:   I planted a Group 4 soybean variety which doesn't mature
        early. The neighbor I bought those soybeans off of wondered
        what in the world I was going to do with Group 4 soybeans.
        That's a variety you plant in Southern Illinois. They had to
        special order them for me.

G28:   We picked an area that couldn't be seen very easily. And, on
        the one side where it possibly could have been seen, we
        planted some corn.

        There were several farmers in the study for whom any advantage they
had from knowing about growing plants was more than compensated for by
their naiveté at avoiding detection. Several were caught because they planted
their marijuana in rows, often along with corn, which turned brown in late
summer while the marijuana was still a bright green. Under these conditions,
the plants were particularly easy to see from the air.

Q: Did you do anything to reduce your risk of being caught by
        the police?
G07:   I had the marijuana screened. I had corn planted on each
        side, so you couldn't see the marijuana very well. I did an
        exceptionally good job on my plants. Unfortunately, my corn
        grew to be six-foot tall and my marijuana plants were about
        fourteen-feet tall.

Q: It doesn't do much good then, does it?
G07:   No, I was just stupid.

G22:   One mistake we made I realized after I saw the aerial pictures
        they took from roughly 1,000 feet. If you were to grow along
        the edge of timber or something, it would be almost impossi-
        ble to distinguish between the plants and the trees. But with
        us, the plants were in a cornfield.
Q: That's fine when the corn is green and the marijuana is small.
G22:   When the corn is green and the plants are green, it all looks
        the same from 1,000 feet. But the corn turned brown and the
        plants were still green and so it was kind of like a neon sign.
        It was just unbelievable when I see the pictures.
Q: Some people said they were growing the plants in straight
        rows.
G22:   That's mainly what we did. I planted the corn down on the
        farm. I just went back in and cut out the corn plants right in
        the row. I planted the marijuana right in the row where the
        corn was.

For those who did take precautions before their arrest, the emphasis
was on hiding the plants and on minimizing contacts with other people. Over
the period covered in this study (1980–1990), there seemed to be an increasing
concern about patterning the plants to avoid aerial detection and to minimize
losses from thieves who might stumble across the plants. This meant growing
the plants in small clusters scattered over a wide area, rather than grouped
together in open fields. It also meant planting marijuana so that it blended in
with other natural plants in the area.

G09:   I spread the plots around. You also just make it grow into
        the environment where it's supposed to be, where it looks
        natural. And you prune it, that's about all. And watching,
        who does what, who owns what land, and whatever.

G02:   Camouflage was my main concern, putting the plants in tree
        areas or shrubbery areas, or anything to break the outline.
        You just don't plant them all together because you know it
        has a very conspicuous color. You get a healthy marijuana
        plant and in the noonday sun, it's fluorescent practically. It's
        just like walking past a fluorescent light, lime-green bright.
        And it's impossible to miss if you know what you are looking
        for.

G23:   If you are going to grow a large amount, you should be growing on the south side of the tree line. You don't grow on the north side. It gets more sun. I think it's a lot harder to spot from an airplane.

Q: Because of the way the shadows hit?

G23:   Right. I know that where the pot was there were airports not very far away. Planes would fly over constantly all day. Even the red and white planes, I know they were spotter planes for the DCI [Illinois State Police Department of Criminal Investigation]. Shit, they never did spot it by air. So if they didn't spot that many plants [about 800], they aren't going to spot twenty or thirty plants.

Secrecy was a theme that ran throughout discussions of avoiding detection. Most growers believed that both theft and arrest were best guarded against by keeping their growing activities secret.

Q: Did you consciously try to keep the number of people you sold to pretty small?

G16:   Oh yeah, certainly. The last few years especially. Years ago, when I first started out, I'd deal with everybody, all the people I knew. After that, I started with just a very few. That's probably what kept me out of trouble. I dealt with some good friends who I went to school with all my life, and I didn't deal with anybody else.

Q: If you were to get back into the business, what would you do differently?

G06:   I wouldn't tell anybody that I was doing it, and I would have it very well hidden. I would tie the plants down, and plant flowers or something to disguise them.

G09:   Well, I wouldn't be married, I'd ride alone. The main thing is just to keep to yourself and do whatever you have to do. Absolutely let no one else in . . . because if you get anyone else involved, then it's something else to hang you up.

Q: What is the single most effective thing a grower can do to avoid being caught by the police?

G08:   Probably just secrecy, just keep your mouth shut.

G20:   I suggest you button your lip and don't tell anybody you got it. And you had better have it well stashed, because people just seem to know where it is. Don't ask me how, but they can smell it, I think.

Those who were not marijuana users and had little to do with drugs (aside from their growing) often maintained very strict secrecy about their activities. Growers who were users were more likely to talk with friends about growing and freely exchanged tips. They were often careful, however, not to reveal the size or location of their operation. Friends might be caught by the police and tell what they knew. More likely, however, was that friends would either steal the crop themselves or inadvertently reveal its location to others who might steal it. For several growers, secrecy meant not only keeping quiet about their activities but tending their outdoor plants when they would not be noticed.

Q: If somebody wants to grow and not get caught, what's the single best thing they can do to keep from getting caught?

G29:   Well, they shouldn't plant it on their own ground. And they should do everything from about 2:00 A.M. to 5:00 A.M. But they have to know which roads to take. But that's when the county sleeps, you know. Because I did jail time and I know how the deputies live. From 2:00 A.M. to 5:00 A.M. they're usually up at the jail eating and sacking out a little while. They get up at 5:00 A.M., and they get back into their cars.

G07:   They should plant it someplace where nobody knows where it's at. And you should only go and take care of it sporadically at night—things like that.

G01:   I really lived a sheltered life that summer. I didn't go to town that much. I guess I was just looking over my shoulder every five minutes, waiting, expecting it to come. As far as disguises and camouflage or anything else, no.

The principle of maintaining a low profile in their activities also applied to indoor growers. While indoor growing is, in general, harder to detect than outdoor operations, there is still the problem of supplies, energy, and the light given off.

Q: Did you do anything to reduce your risk of being caught by the police?

G10:   No. I just tried to act normal, I guess. Well, I kept the windows covered up so that nobody could look in the house. But somebody could have opened the door to the grow room and walked in.

G17:   When I went out and had the CO_2 cylinders filled, I'd have
         somebody do it for me. And I'd move it in the middle of the
         night. When I ordered seed, I'd have it sent to other places.
         I'd send it to somebody else's house who didn't know what it
         was, because it looks like an envelope. If you order growing
         supplies, it comes in boxes, it isn't marked "growing supplies."
         You can have it sent to your grandma's or aunt's, or whatever.

G18:   I put windows up. I build windmills—they had an article in
         National Geographic on how to build portable windmills out
         of water pipe, right out of the house. So, I looked it up, got
         a generator out of a great big old semitruck, and made my
         own generator. I had to cut some power, some kilowatts. I
         put in my little fan which works in only 1.8-mph wind.

G21:   A grower should just keep it secret if they can—not tell any-
         body. Also, when they make purchases of equipment and
         supplies, they should go about it as secretively as they can.
         When they buy soil, they ought to buy it in the summertime.
         I was going down to the nurseries in the middle of winter and
         buying massive quantities of soil and supplies, which looks
         peculiar. I know people here lately who drive up to Chicago
         and buy equipment, just so they avoid any records whatsoever.

         The rural environment itself was a factor in concealing their activities.
In the smaller communities strangers were not trusted. One grower was asked
how difficult it would be to obtain the seeds and knowledge to get started in his
community.

G07:   Well, probably a little harder out here in the sticks than it
         would be in town—you know, in the city. Out here everybody
         knows everybody. You know if somebody like you showed up
         and started hanging out at the bar or something, and started
         asking people to sell you a bag of reefer, you'd soon get your
         ass trashed. That's what would happen.

         In general, police informants were drawn from the local community,
though there were exceptions to this. Growers who were particularly desperate
for money or who were not marijuana users (and thus knew few potential
buyers in the community) were probably more likely to take risks with those
they knew little about.
         The concern these growers had with secrecy was well founded. Nearly
all of the growers in this study were identified through informants. Aerial

surveillance was seldom useful in locating plots, although it was frequently used to verify tips from informants. Although the objective effectiveness of aerial surveillance in finding new plots may be in doubt, this is not to say the technique isn't valuable from a law-enforcement point of view. First, fly-overs seem to have a strong deterrent effect. A number of growers mentioned concern about being detected in this way. Second, fly-overs were useful for the police by providing a shield for their informants. By reporting the detection of a plot as the result of a routine fly-over, it was unnecessary for officials to even acknowledge the existence of an informant. For example, one grower was arrested for having thirteen plants, and these plants were ostensibly discovered in a fly-over. The charges against him were by weight, rather than number and he was inadvertently included in the sampling pool. As it turned out, his operation was much larger than thirteen plants, and it is unlikely that the fly-over was anything but a confirmatory exercise based on an informant's tip.

G14:   They said they were flying over in an airplane, but I don't think that's true. I think they got some inside information from somebody.

Q: So they probably knew where to look?

G14:   Yeah. The plants they caught me with were in a garden spot, but there were more, just two hundred feet from my house, bigger patches that they didn't see.

Q: How many would you guess you had all together, counting the other plants you weren't caught with?

G14:   The other spots had, I don't know, probably over a thousand plants. Because I had over ten spots and there were probably over one hundred plants in each spot.

In summary, most growers recognized the importance of avoiding detection by both thieves and the police. The most important tool for avoiding detection was secrecy. Growers realized, though sometimes not until after their arrest, that almost anyone who knew about the operation was a potential threat. In addition to secrecy, growers were generally sensitive to the importance of avoiding suspicious activities and dispersing their crops over a wide area in such a way that the marijuana plants blend in with other natural foliage.

VIOLENCE IN THE MARIJUANA INDUSTRY

Violence in the drug business makes for good press and this is no less true when the drug is marijuana. When the study began, national magazine accounts gave the impression that many of the growers would be heavily armed and booby traps would be common. The researcher was warned on several occasions, by those with no direct knowledge of the marijuana industry, of the risks he would face interviewing growers. This public image has been fueled in 1991 when a marijuana grower (and cocaine smuggler) became the first person ever sentenced to death under the tough federal drug laws of the late 1980s ("First death sentence," 1991).

In reality, violence was rare among these growers. This was not simply based on the accounts of growers and on public accounts of their arrest but was confirmed in interviews with law-enforcement officials. When asked whether having marijuana growers in the community made it more dangerous to live there, one police officer responded:

P04:   I don't think so. . . . But, as far as the average mentality of a
        marijuana grower or seller goes, we've seen deals consummat-
        ed for half a million dollars with a handshake. If the guy rips
        him off, he just doesn't deal with him anymore. . . . It's totally
        different than cocaine. You know, a guy will front you with
        an ounce of cocaine; he wants to know where you live, where
        your mother lives, where your kids go to school, and he's
        going to kill them all if you don't pay him his money. . . . It
        [cocaine] tends to draw more violent people. But every one
        of those were marijuana users and dealers before they went
        into cocaine.

Other officers emphasized that while the growers themselves were not a violent group, having a locally operated drug business would draw violent people into the community. Realistically, the police must be prepared for the worst-case scenario, but in day-to-day practice they are unlikely to find marijuana growers a physically dangerous group. As will be seen in chapter 9, there are other states in which violence by marijuana growers is more frequent. In general, it appears that growers simply reflect the level of existing violence in an area, rather than introducing violence to an otherwise peaceful region.

The fact that growers did not generally exercise violence did not mean they were immune to it. Violence was a concern of many growers. During the course of questioning, they were asked about their concerns with violence, either from the police or from thieves.

Violence from the Police

In many cases, arrests were made by teams of heavily armed police. Despite this substantial show of force and weaponry, very few growers feared police violence, believing that so long as they cooperated with the arresting officers they would be treated well. This proved to be true in most cases. Several growers did feel threatened by the police, but it was unclear whether the threats were real or perceptions shaped by the tension of the moment.

Q: Were you worried about the police using violence against you?
G26:   A little bit. At the very beginning they said it would go a lot
            easier on me if I cooperated. I took that to imply either a
            physical threat against me or just a threat against my proper-
            ty—they would tear things up.

G22:   Yeah. That night when they arrested me, I wasn't very sure.
            They were very nervous and jumpy. They didn't have regular
            police weapons. They had a couple of uzis, or something like
            that. They had riot-style shotguns and things like that and
            they were real nervous.

G17:   Well, I had never been in that situation before and you see
            stuff on TV and that. And they are pulling guns out and
            pointing them at you. If they knew anything about me, I've
            never owned a gun in my life. I've never had a gun card. I've
            never had a weapon of any kind in my house whatsoever,
            except for kitchen knives or something like that. And it just
            made me think they were getting just a little overboard on
            their authority. But I wasn't really afraid.

For the most part, there was no evidence of violence by the police
against growers. The only documented "abuse" of these growers by the police
was minor, isolated, and unlikely to fit even the most inclusive definition of the
term.

G07:   Well, at one point, the one deputy is a wise ass. There was a
            spade there, and he picked it up and chomped it down in the
            middle of one of my tomato plants, cut one of my plants in
            half. That pissed me off, you know, so I grabbed it and just
            moved it. He started going for his gun, and I guess he
            thought I was going to take a spade to him. There were like
            six cops there, you know, a bunch of cops. But this guy's just
            a deputy, and the county sheriff was real good. I mean, he just
            stepped in between us and said, "Both of you guys just cool it."

Of course, several growers felt they had not been given a fair shake by
the system, but the police were exceptionally professional in their conduct, and
most growers realized that. When growers were angry it was often, not because
of the fact of their arrest, but because of the way it was conducted. This has
also been observed by Erickson (1980) in her study of people arrested for
marijuana possession. One grower with no prior experience with the law was
televised during his arrest and made several statements about the high degree

of professionalism shown by the police and the pride citizens should feel for them.

Violence from Thieves

While growers could feel confident that the police would play by the rules, they had no such assurances from thieves.

Q: Did you worry very much about possible violence either from people who were going to steal your crop or other growers, or the police?

G02:   I wasn't worried about the police at any time, as far as violence was concerned. Because I know the bottom line there is you do what they say when they arrest you and you're cool. But with growers or criminals, the real criminal element is what I call them, the people who will take what they want with violence, yeah, I was worried about them. I always kept loaded guns in the house.

Q: Were you concerned about the possibility of violence from either the police or other growers or people who might try to steal the crop?

G04:   I wasn't concerned about violence from the police. After people started stealing it, then I became concerned about violence from them. I didn't like what was going on, you know. I was concerned that somebody was going to break into my house thinking there was a big stash there or something like that, which there wasn't. I was concerned about violence from the poachers.

The only case that involved gunplay occurred when a grower was target shooting on his land and stumbled upon several teenagers stealing his crop. He said he was outraged that young people were gaining access to his marijuana and made them lay down on the ground to question them about whether they were selling it to other kids. In the confusion of the moment his gun discharged into the shoulder of one of the teenagers. He immediately took the youth to the hospital himself, where he was arrested.

Although most growers in the study had sport weapons, and several were avid hunters, shooting seldom occurred during arrests or in disputes between growers and thieves. This makes more sense when one considers the meaning of guns in a rural context, where most growing occurred.

The Role of Guns

There was simultaneously an absence of violence and a presence of weapons, and this can partly be accounted for by the rural setting in which growing takes place. It is the issue of weapons where the definition of violence used by the law and that used by growers differed. In urban areas firearms are carried with one main target in mind, other people. Of the growers who did not have guns in their houses at the time of the arrest, most lived in larger communities. In rural areas, however, guns have a very different meaning and a variety of other applications. They are commonly carried when traveling in remote areas for the purpose of shooting varmints, hunting, and general target practice. State and federal laws regarding carrying firearms during the commission of a crime (such as cultivating marijuana) are generally based on an urban definition of the function of personal weapons. Growers who carried weapons into the field for sport sometimes faced additional weapons charges, and everyone with felony charges faced the loss of their firearm registration cards after their conviction.

Q: You said you had a gun just for sport?
G23:   We would always go out and shoot by the creek [near the patch]. We had a couple of cows down there, and some hogs.
Q: So you weren't carrying the gun for self-defense?
G23:   No. They asked me that too. I said, "Hell, I spent a year in Vietnam. I carried an M16 and a grenade-launcher there. Why would I carry a 25 automatic pistol in a tight pair of jeans if I was going to protect myself? I would have carried it in my hand." So, they don't use common sense.

Despite their fondness of guns for recreational purposes, some growers tried to avoid trouble by making certain they were unarmed when they tended their crops. Others made it clear that the possibility of violence gave them pause about their growing activities.

Q: Were you concerned about the possibility of violence from people who would steal your crop or from the police?
G22:   No. Because we never carried weapons when we went down there.
Q: You didn't feel the need to protect yourself?
G22:   No. It wasn't worth it. I mean it was worth a lot of money, but it wasn't worth shooting somebody over it.

G10:   Yeah, I was, because one, the guy on that farm down there had an old junk car parked there. He said if anybody tried to rip him off, he'd take that car and he'd crash their cars, that's all he had it for, like a demolition car. If anybody came in there, and I was worried about somebody getting hurt, and I think he had a firearm, too, cause I saw him out shooting something one time. That I didn't go for, that's one of the reasons why I got out of it.

Overall, there was little evidence of violence in the cases examined for this study. There was no indication that people prone to violence are drawn to marijuana growing. On the contrary, there was a striking absence of violence considering the dollar amounts involved and the ease with which violence could have been adopted. Not all growers were concerned with violence, but such feelings were common. It was thought that violence would come from thieves, although it was rare for them to prepare for a response in kind. It is likely that any turn toward violence in the domestic marijuana industry would be the result of violent people entering the business and current growers leaving it.

DRUG USE AMONG MARIJUANA GROWERS[1]

It has been argued that while money is an important motivation for people to become commercial marijuana growers, many growers are also driven by pride and self-fulfillment from growing. Given these financial incentives and intrinsic rewards, it might be assumed that marijuana growers are advocates of marijuana use and actively recruit new users. To determine this, growers were asked whether (1) growing is immoral, (2) legal restrictions on marijuana should be lifted, and (3) marijuana is a harmful drug. In addition, they were asked about their use of other drugs and the involvement of commercial marijuana growers in the distribution of other drugs. All of the growers were asked about these issues, but only the comments of those twenty-seven who admitted their involvement in growing are included in this discussion. Three of the four who denied growing claimed no drug use at all, and the fourth claimed only occasional marijuana use.

Is Growing Marijuana Immoral?

Most growers (20 of 27) did not see their activity as morally wrong, often comparing marijuana with alcohol or tobacco. One grower observed that despite the extensive legal trouble his arrest had caused, including a stay in a federal prison and in a drug treatment center, he could find no one who could give him a satisfactory explanation of why marijuana was illegal and alcohol was legal. Several others echoed these sentiments, while acknowledging that their views were not those of mainstream society.

Q: While you were growing, did you think of what you were doing as morally wrong?

G21:   In the view of mainstream society, yes. But among my kinds of people, no.

Q: You thought it was legally wrong but not morally wrong?

G21:   Yeah. There's a lot of straight people who don't care about people getting high. It's whatever your life is. Some people drink too much and I don't look at them as being morally wrong.

G10:   No, absolutely not. It is not morally wrong. I can show you passages in the Bible, Genesis 122, "I give you all the seeds of herb for meat." . . . All the plants that mankind has been given are supposed to be eaten, whether you smoke it or eat it. You are not altering the chemical. Wine was accidentally discovered because it has the mold that takes the place of the yeast, and the water was changed into wine at the wedding in the Bible. There's a lot of religious people that still think that anything that injures your body is immoral, but I don't believe it injures your body that much.

A few argued that growing was morally justifiable because of their considerable economic need or because of a belief that the government had other, more pressing concerns.

G12:   I didn't have any money. I was broke. I knew it was wrong, but I went ahead and did it because I needed some cash.

G24:   I think if I hadn't gotten into farming I probably wouldn't have grown marijuana. I do know I started farming at the wrong time. I bought land at the wrong time. When I was arrested I was over $300,000 in debt and had assets of probably $80,000. . . . Looking back at it I probably could have just thrown up my hands and told the creditors, "Sorry boys." To me that's more morally wrong than growing marijuana.

G02:   I don't really know what would be the social impact of tearing down laws as far as marijuana is concerned. I'm concerned about that, of course, but in retrospect I figure the ultimate destruction of society has already occurred to this nation when the Supreme Court justified the death of the unborn. So, from a social impact and a moral point of view, I cannot even

consider smoking a joint any harm to this nation when unborn
children are slaughtered.

Overall, the positions argued by these growers read like a list of
Matza's (1964) "techniques of neutralization."   Matza's techniques are
rationalizations used by offenders to justify their actions, by arguing either that
the law is wrong or that it is right in principle but is not applicable to their
situation.

Despite their willingness to talk in depth about other aspects of their
business, growers had relatively little to say about the morality of their
activities. It appeared that most growers didn't spend much time agonizing
over the morality of their actions.

G18:   I've got good morals. If and when I ever die, and I go to hell,
         the only reason I'll go to hell is for drugs. That would be the
         only reason. For any other reason, I'll go to heaven. That
         would be the only reason they'd send me to hell, just for
         drugs.

G04:   Yes, that was always a conflict I had. I thought there were
         two sides to it. The bad side was that nobody should do
         drugs, and I was feeding addictions by giving people marijua-
         na. Other than that, I didn't see all that much wrong with it.
         I knew it was illegal, but I didn't feel that every law we have
         is correct.

Lifting Legal Restrictions on Marijuana

Having been subject to the force of the law, it is not surprising that
many growers favored easing legal restrictions on marijuana. What was
surprising was the lack of consensus on this and the limits they would place on
decriminalization. Most favored less-harsh legal restrictions on marijuana use
and cultivation, but nearly all wanted strict government regulation of marijuana,
including minimum age restrictions.

G13:   I don't believe you ought to smoke a big snoot full and go to
         work. . . . I would hate to see it readily available to children.
         Of course, alcohol is too, and I hate that too. It ought to be
         regulated for sure.

G08:   If they would legalize it, they probably should do it as they do
         alcohol. . . . I think they should have a regulation on it—age

limit, amount, and public use. I just don't see anything illegal about sitting on a porch and smoking a joint.

G24:   I'd like to see the government treat it like tobacco—you could only grow so much. It would certainly help the farming economy. I certainly don't think teenagers should use it. Although I'm sure teenagers would.

G16:   They'd have to control it in some way, I suppose, so kids can't get it.

A few growers believed that strict legal restrictions should be kept as a way to deter people from entering the business.

G18:   Keep it illegal. That will throw a lot of people away from it.

G12:   Always keep it illegal, but . . . give more people probation, strict probation. It will save a lot of taxpayer's money. Then if they screw up, then they go in [to prison].

G01:   I think we should keep current penalties, because if marijuana is legalized, it should be grown by either the government or subcontracted to farmers who know what they are doing. This is something you are putting into your body. Some idiot could lace it with something, or spike it, or leave chemical residues on it. If it was made available to the public, it should be like alcohol after prohibition. It should be grown by somebody who has got their head on their shoulders.

The most common response to questions about legalization was that legal penalties should be eased but not eliminated. There was considerable worry about teenagers having too much access to marijuana and about heavy use by some people. The level of concern about teenagers obtaining marijuana may seem surprising but makes more sense when it is remembered that most growers were in their late thirties, and several had teenagers of their own. One grower rather vividly illustrates how these conflicting feelings were sometimes played out.

Q: So your children didn't know about your marijuana growing?
G04:   No, well they suspected. I was not one of those people who smoked reefer in the house in front of the kids or anything. I always kept it away from them, because I really didn't feel it was right. I smoked frequently, but I always smoked outside. I didn't smoke in front of them. And I always told

them it was wrong, they shouldn't do it. And I was usually
high when I told them that.

This view was echoed by one official, who had been doing undercover work for
fifteen years.

P30:   Now what I'm seeing is that a lot of these growers have kids
          who are 16–17 years old, and these adults are growing it in
          their basements where the kids are not even allowed to go.
          And they can't understand why their kids are now doing
          drugs. They've got a real conflict between growing and their
          ideals of what they want their children to be.

Concern about marijuana being available to young people was also
reported in Erickson's (1989) study of adult marijuana users. Ironically, in both
her study and this one, adults favored using the law to limit access to marijuana
by teens, even though the law had not deterred their own adult activities and,
in some cases, their own purchases of marijuana when they were adolescents.

The Harm from Marijuana Use

Most users either saw no physical harm in moderate marijuana use or,
more commonly, believed that the harm was real and potentially serious, but
no greater than from tobacco or alcohol.

G12:   You smoke enough pot and you'll forget things. You know,
          you're supposed to go get something, or supposed to turn
          here or go there. I think it screws you up. Alcohol does the
          same thing to you, but it's legal.

G08:   Well, I don't feel it's too harmful. I've smoked marijuana for
          over twenty years. I don't look like I've been harmed too
          much by it. I don't smoke a joint and go out in the yard and
          say, "What am I going to do now?"

G04:   Well, I believe it's harmful. I can't imagine it being beneficial.
          Just like cigarettes. I don't believe there is anything beneficial
          about cigarettes. I've never heard of anything that was
          beneficial to the body from smoking marijuana.

G21:   I think cigarettes are twice as harmful as pot. Alcohol is four
          times as harmful.

G12:   It will harm you. I believe alcohol will harm you more. I felt
        worse when I went out and drank a fifth of Jack Daniels than
        I did when I smoked five joints or something, when I woke up
        the next morning.

G22:   If someone smoked as much marijuana as they did tobacco,
        then I suppose it would be more harmful. But I think tobacco
        is going to end up killing a lot more people than marijuana is.

It was also common for growers to make a distinction between heavy
and moderate marijuana use. In moderation, marijuana was seen as doing little
harm. Heavy regular use was a different matter.

G16:   It's no different from alcohol. In moderate amounts it isn't
        that bad, but it's just like anything. If you overdo anything,
        it's going to hurt your body.

G22:   It just depends. If they are smoking once a week, twice a
        week, or something like that, then no, I don't think it's
        extremely harmful to them. But I have seen some guys who
        smoked every day. I can tell it has done something to them.
        They have lost some brain cells somewhere along the line.

G24:   Obviously if you smoke ten marijuana cigarettes a day and
        keep yourself locked in your room, you'll become a vegetable.
        It's just not good for you. But if you can function well in
        society and smoke a little bit at a party on a weekend or
        smoke it when you get home from work with your beer, I
        don't see any difference.

Almost all growers in this study had tried marijuana (26 of 27) and
about half were daily users in the month prior to their arrest. A few had only
tried marijuana once or twice after they began growing it, to see what it was
like. Most used marijuana rather frequently. Despite this pattern of use, they
recognized the potential harm from marijuana, particularly regular heavy use.

Other Drugs

Most who had used marijuana had also tried other drugs. They were
asked whether they had ever used marijuana, hashish, cocaine, PCP, LSD,
heroin, amphetamines, and mushrooms. Nineteen of the twenty-seven subjects
who admitted growing reported having ever tried four or more illegal
substances, most commonly hashish, cocaine, amphetamines, and LSD. Their

pattern of substance abuse at the time of the arrest was not asked, although remarks made during the interviews suggested that for many the active use of other drugs was a phase that had passed by the time of their arrest.

Only one of these commercial growers admitted being involved in the large-scale dealing of imported marijuana and other drugs. Ironically, marijuana cultivation did not lead to his involvement with other aspects of the drug business, but followed it. Another grower had purchased quarter-pounds of marijuana prior to growing, but marijuana cultivation led him to cut down on his interactions with marijuana importers.

Q: So getting involved in growing actually led you to cut back on
        dealing [in marijuana]?
G21:   That's true. I know it did. Before I started growing I'd buy
        at least a quarter-pound every time because it's cheaper that
        way. And then out of that quarter-pound I'd sell at least half
        of it to make a little money to recoup the price and buy
        another quarter-pound. That made it cheaper. I'd buy a
        large quantity to make the price cheaper for me and then sell
        a little more and make it cheaper yet. Once I started growing
        I gave away a lot to close friends that was just as good as the
        commercial stuff they were paying for on the street. I just
        gave that stuff away.

Overall, there was no evidence that entering commercial marijuana growing enticed people to enter other aspects of the drug business or gave them the contacts they needed to make the transition. It is not simply that marijuana growers lacked the opportunity to deal in other drugs; they probably could have made such connections if they had tried. What seemed to keep most growers out of dealing in other drugs were feelings that enough money could be made from marijuana, that marijuana was very different from other drugs, and that the rewards from growing marijuana could not be duplicated by simply distributing other drugs.

Q: Do people say, "If I can make this much from marijuana, I
        can make more from some other drug?"
G28:   Of the guys who I know who were involved in growing, no.
        The real, true grower, he's satisfied growing it. You know, it's
        like the moonshiners made their whiskey. They could have
        turned around and made some wine and sold that too, but
        they just never did. They were satisfied to make the one
        thing. And the true marijuana growers probably still are.
        Now, that's not 100 percent by any means, but I'd probably
        say the majority.

Most growers saw no similarities between the harm from marijuana and that from other drugs. Other drugs were dangerous and marijuana was not, a view expressed even by those who had used a variety of other drugs. Very few knew much about heroin; only four had tried it and none were regular users. Cocaine was more common, having been tried by twenty-one of the twenty-seven, and their comments about it were consistently negative.

G17:   I believe cocaine is harmful. I don't think cocaine should ever be legalized in any way, shape, or form. Marijuana is like candy compared to cocaine. I mean, there is no comparison at all.

G23:   Well, they say cocaine is hard on your heart and stuff like that. I have done coke occasionally. I don't think coke is really that harmful. But I have seen people start doing coke, and they would spend money [on coke] that they should use for food and other stuff. And it's not that way with pot. You can deal without having pot.

G18:   Cocaine is a very addicting drug. It's a damaging drug. It will take people away without them even knowing it.

G28:   Cocaine is really an abuser and a killer. Marijuana is considered more like a cigarette; even though it's going to kill you, it's going to be a long time.

G10:   I used to mess around with cocaine. You'll go out of your way to find money to buy that, but not pot. That's how I quit using cocaine, I just started smoking pot. Back then it was just cocaine, that's all I wanted. And then a friend of mine says, "Hey, why are you wasting your money on that?" Pot wasn't that expensive. And when you smoke pot, you just smoke one joint. You're high and you don't necessarily want any more; cocaine you want to keep doing it, stay up all night and go on and on. My own belief is that the best way to get people off cocaine in the United States would be to legalize pot.

Though not frequently reported in this study, the suggestion in the preceding quote that marijuana may facilitate the termination of cocaine use has been noted elsewhere. In their study of active cocaine users, Erickson and Murray (1989) found that among those who reported an interest in stopping or moderating their cocaine use, there was no corresponding interest in terminating the use of marijuana:

Cocaine lacks the social integration, acceptability, and ease of
access accorded to cannabis and is perceived to pose greater
legal and health risks. . . . While so much of the current drug
literature has emphasized the progression from cannabis to
cocaine, we had apparently unearthed an example of "de-
escalation." (149, 151)

The possibility that marijuana may serve as a gateway *out* of the use of other
drugs is important and worth further study.

In making sense of the comments by these growers, it must be
remembered that many were sentenced to drug treatment or went through a
drug treatment program after their arrest in the hope of gaining leniency from
the judge. It is unknown how many had their views changed as a result of this
experience. For example, several indicated that as a result of treatment they
had come to think of marijuana as addicting and of drug use as destructive.
This is clearly illustrated in the comments by growers in the next section on the
impact of the arrest.

In summary, most of these growers did not see their activities as
morally wrong but realized that others might feel differently. Many were users
and most had at least tried other drugs. Although they could justify the
morality of their growing to themselves, they were less certain about the
wisdom of legalizing marijuana. Most thought that legal penalties should be
reduced but that strict government controls should be in place. They were
particularly interested in keeping marijuana out of the hands of teenagers,
although many had no way of preventing this from happening with their own
crops. Finally, there seems to be little overlap between the business of growing
marijuana and the business of trafficking in other drugs, at least in Illinois at
this time. Growers made a distinction between their marijuana cultivation and
"real" drug dealing. If we take these growers at their word, it seems unlikely
that most of the growers interviewed for this study would have ever moved into
trafficking in cocaine or heroin.

THE ARREST AND ITS IMPACT

Growers were asked about both the positive and the negative impact
of the arrest. Their responses provide insights into their social networks, the
nature of their ties to the local community, and the deterrent effects of the
arrest. Comments on the negative consequences suggested there were three
major areas in which the arrest made an impact: reputation, family, and work.

Damage to Their Reputation

One of the more common responses, particularly by growers who had been lifelong residents and had no prior arrests, was that their reputation in the community had been damaged. In small rural communities, this can be a serious consequence.

Q: The arrest has clearly caused you some problems. Overall, what would you say has been the worst thing that has occurred because of your arrest? That is, what has happened to you as a result of your arrest that you most regret?

G01:   Being put down for a federal conviction really puts you down into a deep hole. I've had to scratch, and claw, and dig, and try to repair what's left of the family name. And it's made me a lot hungrier for success than before my conviction. So, I have to prove to all these people that I'm not a piece of dirt lowlife, I am a good person, good man, and an excellent manager. And as soon as I get up to success, then I'd have proved them wrong.

G08:   Probably the publicity and the personal effect of it; it still hangs over my head. I'm getting over the money part of it; I mean, everybody gets over the money. For a while I wouldn't even go to town because I just didn't even want to be in town, people looking at you and staring at you. I don't like for people to think that I'm a criminal. For a long time, I wouldn't even go into the local IGA store, it's that type of community. If they were to go to New York and see the homeless people and these kids twelve-years-old doing crack and some person shooting at another one, why they wouldn't believe it. So I just figured, well, I'll just have to go with the flow. So I'm a criminal, and they'll just have to think whatever they think. But it took me a while to get used to that pattern of people thinking you're that bad.

G11:   The fact that I had a good reputation; I worked all my life for this reputation and my standing in the community, and then to just be laughed at. And I am so disappointed at our legal system; it is such a joke.

G27:   Probably the things that the prosecutor said bothered me. ... The courtroom was full that day, and a lot of people from our neighborhood were there, a lot of people from the town were there. . . . It was the first time that anybody had ever said things like that. There's one person standing up there in front of everybody saying all that bad stuff about you . . . well, that hurt.

Despite the embarrassment, few had moved from their communities or planned to in the future. Many emphasized the importance of working hard to reestablish their good name. Several were particularly offended by the efforts of the police and prosecutor to build a case against them by, in their view, distorting the truth.

G28:   Probably the biggest thing that upset me was the snitching, and the deceitfulness of the government, and the lying. I didn't like the snitching, but I lived with that. But when they were telling on me, they were making up things and lying to make them look better in the government's eye. Well, the government feeds them that information and tells them to say that. And a lot of that was done in my case. When I read the testimony against me, a third of the stuff they said was absolutely the truth, a third of it was just right out lies, and a third of it I didn't know anything about. I didn't like that.

Harm to Their Family

Other growers emphasized not only their personal shame, but the impact it had on their family and their relationship with their family. In some cases the arrest led to the breakup of the family. In other cases it introduced strain among family members.

Q: What is the thing you regret most about the arrest?
G05:   Mainly what it did to my reputation, also what it did to my family. It split us up; I'm from a large family, it split our family completely up.

G09:   Loss of control of my child. It's affecting me. . . . Everything else, I dealt with it; it's the only thing that's bothered me worse, losing my child. [He divorced while in prison and lost custody of his child.]

G20A: It alienated me from my son. He's not quite my son any more like he used to be, and that bothers me a great deal.

G20B: The worst thing has been the deterioration of my children. Because I was not available to them at a time they really needed me. They pressured the kids, and the kids didn't need the pressure.

G21:   The separation between me and my girlfriend.

G29:   Probably the divorce, losing my kids. She wanted me to move up there [to another community], but you can't get away from your problems, and I was born and raised here.

It is one thing to suffer for one's own poor judgment; it is another to see the consequences fall on people you love. For several of the growers any personal shame they felt was easy to deal with compared with seeing family members put through public humiliation.

G14:   Probably how it reflected back on my children mostly. . . . Cause everybody wants to know, "Well, where is your dad?" "Well, he's in prison." I feel bad that they had to go through it. Everything else I could cope with.

G15:   The embarrassment to my parents and to my wife. The financial burden it put on us through having to hire attorneys for legal defense. I think that for the most part, I feel more of the embarrassment and all that for them, than they felt for themselves. Because I was responsible. They didn't ask to be brought into the situation, and at the time, I was unaware of what the repercussions would really be for them.

G22:   What it did to my family. It was very hard on them the time I was in prison. They were very good about coming and visiting. They were down almost every other weekend. But it was very hard on the relationship between my wife and I. She had to learn to do for herself while I was gone. It's hard just to turn around when I come home and have everything be the same as when I left.

G23:   My family, mostly. Just being associated with drugs, because everybody is coming down on drugs. Some of them don't understand it.

G24:   I suppose it was the harm it caused to my mother. I can get over that how it bothered me. It caused her quite a bit of anguish.

G30:   The impact on my wife and my kid. You know, the fact that
         they had people look down on them.

Impact on Work and Money

     Overall, the impact of the arrest on a grower's reputation and family
was considerable.   Several growers also emphasized the more tangible
consequences of a drug arrest, noting its impact on their ability to find work.
In rural counties where unemployment is often high, finding a job with a clean
arrest record can be difficult. A drug arrest can make finding a job nearly
impossible and is a continuous reminder of their damaged reputations.

Q: What is the thing you regret most about your arrest?
G17:   Having two felonies on my record. That would probably be
         the worst thing. It hasn't kept me from getting a good job;
         I'm thankful that I did run across a good job, I just lucked
         out. I went a long time without any work. Money would be
         the second worst thing; losing my [old] job would be third.
         Losing some respect from your family, I mean, they stuck
         behind me the whole time and everything, but they think a
         little bit less of me, especially my grandparents. My mom and
         dad, they're fairly young, and the main thing to them is as
         long as I don't do it again, keep working, stay out of trouble,
         that's what impresses them the most right now.   But my
         grandparents, aunts and uncles, they keep that in the back of
         their heads; it ain't that they look at you with disgust, but you
         know that it bothers them.

G01:   The disgrace of a federal conviction, and its consequences; I'm
         ineligible for any kind of government programs, farm pro-
         grams. I could have had a farm today, with my name on it, if
         it hadn't been for that. County supervisor told me flat out,
         "Well, after it's over [probation], come and see me, and we'll
         see what we can do." I have to be patient.

G02:   I would say the worst thing is on any real future in a job. It
         seems that if you know somebody, you can get good work. If,
         of course, that person trusts you as a good worker. You've
         got to be able to influence them enough that they'll say, "Hey,
         come on in here." They'll have a million applicants, they
         know you. "I know your work; you'll do the job; you're hired."
         But the stigma of being a drug felon is pretty deep these days,
         pretty deep. It's not as bad as being a child abuser, but

sometimes it's close. But as more and more people are arrested, and as the generation grows older, I'm sure that the stigma will fall off.

G04: The punishment from the law wasn't that hard to take; I had no trouble while on probation. The loss of my job was probably the worst thing that had happened. Of course, it's embarrassing to get busted, but getting arrested probably did me a lot of good.

G06: The financial side of it really. The other part of it . . . I wanted to have a strong backbone about this and say, "Hey, I can be a pot smoker and still be a damn good person," but it's like a stigma. Still, I don't believe that pot smoking is wrong, and I try to stand up for that, so I guess the financial part is the worst part.

G07: Well, I lost my contract with the city and the county for a year and a half. That was a big financial burden for me, because that's half my income right there. And then it upset my wife pretty bad. That's probably the two worst things. The jail time, hell, a bullshit county jail like that, you can do that standing on your head.

G10: Well, letting down my friends has probably been the worst. But financially it's been the most devastating in that area. It about wrecks your business. In a big city, it probably wouldn't have made a difference. But in a small town, with profession-al people where you deal one on one with the same people all the time, it has a big effect. A lot of people say, "You should move out of here, this is a Peyton Place, and people will never forget." That's my goal; I may move away eventually, but I'm bound and determined to get my reputation back.

G12: I'm losing my farm operation.

G13: The first thing that comes to mind is money, but that seems kind of trashy, doesn't it? I lost a promotion definitely, and almost lost my job. I lost my self-confidence for a while.

G31: I don't have a good answer for that, because there's several things that are equally tough. I think about the money. And I think about the things that I have to do without because I don't have the money. I think about the things that it did to me mentally and physically. I think about how it made the rest of my family feel. I think about the whole system and how I got caught up in it. But I mostly think about the money. Because to me, at this point in life, money is happiness, and if we don't have the money to do the things we want to do, and I'm even talking about buying food, then we're unhappy people.

While many offenders saw the arrest as a catastrophic event, there were a few on whom it had little impact. These were generally the minority of growers who had prior records and whose public identity had already been tainted. Whether the effects were severe or minor, many growers also saw positive consequences of the arrest, an issue to which the discussion now shifts.

Positive Consequences of Arrest

Despite prison, heavy fines, damage to their reputation, and other problems that arose from their arrest, almost two-thirds of these growers were able to see something positive coming from the arrest. These positive experiences fit into several categories. The most common was a reduction in their drug use and a corresponding change in the direction of their life.

Q: Is there anything positive or good that has come out of your arrest?

G02:   Absolutely. Since the conviction I have been looking forward to getting out of drugs, to staying completely away from them, to leave them behind, to get on with my life.

G04:   I managed to get my life turned around because of that. And I started to go to college. I see a lot more hope. I figure the reason I was growing reefer is because I was smoking it, and I was smoking it because I was depressed. I needed to get out of the situation I was in, and getting arrested got me out of that situation. . . . I'm assuming I'm eventually going to be able to get a job. If I can't get a job because of being arrested. . . . it's not going to be beneficial. But I think in the long run it will be.

G05:   Well, I can't really think of anything other than I've never done any drugs of any kind since I've been arrested. . . . I really don't miss them. That's one thing I would be doing otherwise, but I haven't; I shy away any time it's even around, cause I'm still on parole, and I just don't have use for it any more. The penalty is too steep.

G10:   It stopped me from getting more and more involved [in marijuana growing]. I could have been involved in something else eventually, if I could have gotten away with that. You know, it turned my life around; that's what's good about it.

G12:   I quit doing drugs.

G14:   Just mostly the simple fact that I learned that it [smoking marijuana] was just a habit. . . . That and I'm trying to get some kind of trade where I can really make it, instead of having to worry about every dollar.

G15:   Well, just the fact that I no longer smoke marijuana. I have broken that addiction. It had me in its grips, I had to have it all the time, I had to have it in my possession. If I started to get low, I had to get more . . . think about where I was going to get more. I'd probably spend at least $50 a week.

G17:   The people I was dealing with quit dealing. Most of the people I associated with at the time quit getting high altogether. Some of them still drink, but most of them quit, especially cocaine, which is real positive because I think it's a dangerous drug. That, and it got me a little bit closer to my family, because before I was caught, I was getting so strung out on cocaine, I wasn't going to family functions, wasn't associating with anybody too much. And now, I'm not using and I'm not getting in trouble, and I'm back with my family and we're talking, and the job I've got now is ten times better than the one I lost.

Others saw the arrest as an event that helped build their self-confidence, either because it taught them to deal with problems or because it gave their life new direction.

G09:   Yeah. After time has gone by, yeah. It helped me. It's pushed me to learn a lot more; it just changed my whole attitude. I hit bottom. I've still got a way to go, but I was able to build myself back up. It probably was best that I did get arrested.

G06:   Yes, after it was all over. I learned a lot about how the law
         works, which I was totally ignorant of before, and I think,
         after it was all over, it helped me build some self-esteem just
         by having to put up with people and what they said. And it
         taught me who my friends were and who my friends weren't.

G21:   I'll be getting into a different profession. I was a welder for
         fifteen years. I just didn't enjoy it any more. In the long run,
         when I get out of here [prison], I plan on driving a truck.
         That's probably the only good thing that will come out of this
         is that I'll switch professions.

G24:   It got me out of farming. It gave me the drive to finish my
         degree, which I started when I graduated from high school.
         At the time, I was going to school just to pacify my parents.
         I really didn't care if I finished or not.

In addition, there were a variety of individual benefits that do not
neatly fit into a single category but for a particular grower may have been very
significant.

G03:   Overall, there are more benefits than losses. It is true I lost
         my farm, but I think of it this way, that I no longer have to
         worry myself and work so hard. These are only material
         things and they will soon pass away from all of us. I have no
         regrets whatsoever, for I have had a good life and the Lord
         has blessed me and my family. I thank the Lord for a
         wonderful life and for taking care of me and my darling wife.

G07:   Well, I joined NORML [National Organization for the
         Reform of Marijuana Laws] after that. I was pretty apathetic
         politically before that, and I changed my views on politics and
         a lot of other things pretty radically since.

G20A: I'm probably closer to my father than I have ever been before.
         And the friends that I have I know are friends now. Some-
         times, no matter how well you know a person, you don't really
         know how good a friend they are; well, I know now. I know
         every friend I've got, believe me. And, before that, I may not
         have been so sure.

G22:   I met a lot of good people. A lot of people don't understand
         until you get involved in something like that. Most of the
         people I met in prison and made friends in there aren't what

you call hardened criminals or anything like that. If you saw them on the street today, you're not going to pick them out and say that guy there is an ex-con or whatever. I just met some real good people.

G28: It brought enough pressure on me that God could get my attention. I found the Lord. Kind of an unusual way, but if that's what it took, fine. I can look at things a lot happier, more positive.

G31: Well, the only thing that's positive about it is knowing that if I ever got into trouble my family and my relations would stick behind me. They wouldn't disown me.

The "benefits" of arrest are not those initially sought by the grower, but are the by-products of a difficult experience. Most of these growers had limited prior exposure to the process or consequences of arrest—only two had ever served time in prison. Consequently, they were ill-prepared for the way the arrest would change their lives. Several were surprised and angered by aggressive prosecutors who painted them as criminals in court and in the press. Prior to the arrest they had not really defined themselves this way, and they were not prepared for others to impose that definition upon them. Because they did not see themselves as "real" criminals, several were surprised and somewhat annoyed that the police would make the arrest using a large number of officers who were heavily armed, as though they were dangerous.

Q: At the time the police came, did you think it was not the police, but somebody coming to steal your crop?
G24: No. They just did it in such a grand scale. They basically had a SWAT team out here to arrest me.
Q: There were quite a few of them?
G24: Oh, bunches of them, over twenty. What I found silly was that all they had to do was have the sheriff knock on the door and say, "X, you are growing marijuana and we have to take you in," instead of wasting all the taxpayers' money on this big publicity stunt. That's the way I look at it.

COMMUNITY RESPONSE TO THE ARREST

In Humboldt County, California, citizens have organized a group called Citizens' Observation Group (COG) designed to monitor marijuana enforcement activity and to warn growers about impending raids (Trebach, 1987; CBS News, 1989). In several states proponents of legalization are political candidates (Kelly, 1990). In Kentucky political parties have formed that advocate legalizing marijuana, and a well-known attorney in the state is running for governor on a legalization platform. There are also scattered reports of citizens cooperating against marijuana enforcement in Kentucky by refusing to sell state troopers gasoline or food (Jehl, 1990). Vermont has also reported an instance in which several hundred local citizens rallied to prevent the sale of a farm seized during a marijuana raid (Johnson, 1989).

During the course of this study, no anti-enforcement groups or local political organizations advocating legalization were reported, either by growers or by law-enforcement officials. What support these growers received after the arrest was individual and based on personal friendship rather than on their status as marijuana growers. Growers could sometimes count on family members for financial assistance, but only a few received offers of such assistance from others. And these offers were based on personal ties.

In Illinois there is little citizen support for marijuana growing, and most arrested growers reported little support or encouragement from local residents following the arrest.

G30:   There were probably four or five people we know who looked
        down on us. . . . But I haven't seen very many people turn
        their backs on us because of it. I'm not saying they condone
        it, but people know me well enough to know that I'm not
        really a bad person. It's just that I made a bad mistake, that's
        all.

Community attitudes toward marijuana growing, as reflected in the treatment of arrested growers, varied from opposition to tolerance, but neither was expressed in public demonstrations. Growers seemed particularly surprised and discouraged by silence or even avoidance by their "friends," and several came to view the arrest as a litmus test of their friendships.

Q: Did your arrest change the way people acted toward you?
G05:   Yes. I think some of them were afraid to be seen with me.
        I don't know if they were thinking of their reputation or what.
        Well, I found out who my real friends were. The people who
        really knew me, I mean really knew me, it didn't change them
        a bit. They were supportive and helpful, and the other
        people, they would just talk behind your back. They wouldn't
        talk in front of me, they'd never come out and accuse me to
        my face.

G20:   Any of my friends who are friends are still friends, and those
        who looked down on me and believed what was in the papers

aren't really my friends to begin with. It gave me a better insight into who is my friend and who isn't.

G22:   Some of the people I thought were friends did [treat me differently]. My real friends didn't.

G29:   You find out, when you get in trouble like that, who's your good friends. I mean, my brother-in-law and sister, they're rednecks like me, but they were really helpful. I was broke and they even bought groceries for us to eat, which was nice. And the church, they even bought groceries for us.

Though not generally receiving support from local citizens, neither did most growers experience overt hostility. The most common response was for citizens to avoid them, and this was as painful for many as a direct confrontation. A few received anonymous telephone calls, but these were few in number and were about as likely to be supportive as critical.

It was originally planned that community members would be interviewed about the effects of the arrest on the local area and to determine the level of support for growing. This turned out to be extremely difficult and after repeated failed efforts, and a few disappointing interviews, was stopped. These problems manifested themselves in several ways. In one of the larger communities (35,000 people), for example, city police were first contacted, but they were reluctant to talk if the interview focused on the community rather than the details of the particular case alone. Their precise reasons were never made clear, but it appeared they were concerned about further tarnishing the image of the community. In smaller communities concern with community image was compounded by a hesitation to speak with outsiders and a concern that the grower or his family would be further embarrassed and hurt by any discussion of the case. This assessment is largely conjecture but fits with our experiences in these communities and with things that were said during the course of finding cases and conducting interviews. Six sheriffs reported they had such cases but were unwilling to provide any names.

The caution shown by these residents is in many ways understandable. Even with assurances of confidentiality, residents and officials from these rural areas did not know the researcher personally and had no way of knowing that their comments would not come back to somehow damage the reputation of the local area. On the positive side, difficulties in obtaining the cooperation of citizens illustrated the power of community in these areas and this, in turn, may have important implications for policies designed to regulate marijuana growing. Of course, a distrust of outsiders is not unique to rural communities, but in rural areas, where the pool of interview subjects is small from the start, the impact on research can be substantial.

SUMMARY

For most growers, avoiding detection often meant a greater emphasis on hiding crops from thieves than from the police. In general, these efforts involved dispersing crops over a wide area in small clusters of plants and having those clusters blend in with existing foliage. Avoiding detection also meant keeping quiet about their growing activities (or at least the scale of those activities), since even friends with whom they smoked were potential thieves or eventual police informants. Secrecy was a persistent theme among these growers, and one consequence of this was that the social and professional networks of growers was quite small. Snowballing techniques used in urban studies of drug users would simply not have been possible with these growers.

Despite the potentially large sums of money involved, there was little evidence of violence among these marijuana growers—an observation supported in police interviews. Such things as booby traps or explosive devices were simply not used in these cases. While growers were not a source of violence, many feared violence from thieves, whose actions were seen as unpredictable.

While a few growers had problems with the morality of their actions, most were able to justify growing to themselves. And, while most favored easing criminal penalties for marijuana, they were not disposed to having marijuana freely available. Nearly all wanted legal restrictions that would keep marijuana away from adolescents. Several had made at least perfunctory efforts to keep their crops from young people, although they must have realized they had only limited control over this activity.

Most growers saw marijuana as harmful but considered it more comparable to alcohol or tobacco than to other illegal drugs. Most had tried a variety of other drugs, usually hashish, cocaine, amphetamines, or LSD, but only a few reported being regular users. In fact, there was general agreement that cocaine was a damaging, addictive drug to be avoided. It did not appear that involvement in marijuana growing led to trafficking in other drugs, although it may have provided the money to purchase other drugs for consumption.

For growers with no prior criminal involvement, the impact of the arrest was substantial—significantly damaging their reputation, impacting their families, and making it difficult to obtain work. For those growers with prior arrests, the impact of an arrest for marijuana cultivation was less significant. While most reported problems as a result of the arrest, most growers also identified positive consequences. These included ending drug use and, in some cases, changing the direction of their lives.

Unlike reported instances from California and Kentucky, there was no evidence of public support for marijuana growers, even in those areas in which growing was most common. What support growers did receive after the arrest was based on personal friendships rather than on their status as marijuana growers. Finally, rural culture imposes some restrictions on research of this type. It was difficult to interview townspeople about the impact of the arrest on the community, and even some rural police were reluctant to speak with outsiders about what they defined as a local problem.

NOTE

1. The discussion of drug use and attitudes toward drugs by marijuana cultivators draws on materials from Weisheit (1991b).

9

A LAW-ENFORCEMENT PERSPECTIVE

The primary focus of this study is on growers, but the input of enforcement officials was important as a means of keeping grower comments in perspective. During the course of the study thirty-three law-enforcement officials familiar with marijuana enforcement were interviewed. Among these officials were county sheriffs, state police, agents of the Drug Enforcement Administration, federal and local prosecutors, and representatives from two national forests.

Twenty of these officials were from Illinois. The remainder were from Indiana, Kentucky, Missouri, Tennessee, and Hawaii. Because growers were primarily from Illinois, the focus is first on Illinois officials. This allows the views of growers and officials to be directly compared. Later in the chapter information from officials in other states will place these findings in a larger context.

Officials were identified through one of three procedures. First, as newspaper stories about arrests for marijuana growing were located, officials identified by name were contacted for an interview. Second, every sheriff and state's attorney in the state, outside of Cook County (which is entirely urban Chicago), was sent a letter inquiring about marijuana cultivation cases in their jurisdiction. Positive responses were followed with a telephone call, and an interview was arranged in cases where the official was agreeable and appeared knowledgeable about marijuana growers. A third avenue by which officials were identified was through snowballing, in which interviewed officials gave the names of others. In general, unsolicited mail contacts were the least fruitful means of locating officials. Press accounts and recommendations from other officials were far more productive.

In many respects, interviewing enforcement officials was frustrating. Although officials were selected who had direct involvement in arresting marijuana growers, or whose job focused primarily on drug enforcement, there was an extremely wide range of knowledge about marijuana growing. The variation in knowledge and amount of experience were so great that adhering to a standardized set of interview questions was nearly impossible.

One of the primary reasons for this variation in knowledge was that marijuana enforcement is only one of many duties facing sheriffs and prosecutors. Even state police officers assigned to drug enforcement are often responsible, not only for marijuana, but for a host of other drugs as well. As a rule, the most informative interviews were those with officials who had a personal curiosity about marijuana cases and had taken it upon themselves to learn as much about them as possible. For example, one of the first interviews was with a sheriff's deputy who was extremely knowledgeable about marijuana growing and marijuana growers. The interview lasted several hours and his comments were valuable in developing the interview instrument for growers and in guiding later interviews with other police officials. At the other extreme were several officials whose interviews were not even tape-recorded because they simply knew too little about the subject. Among sheriffs this sometimes happened because in that county marijuana enforcement had been turned over to the state police. Among state police this sometimes happened because cultivation was not a common problem in their district and was thus given a lower priority than the enforcement of other drugs.

The lack of knowledge about marijuana and marijuana growers is also the product of another reality of drug enforcement. Marijuana arrests and eradication are not accorded the status given arrests for cocaine or heroin. Although state and local resources for drug investigations are considerable, they are finite, and marijuana enforcement must sometimes take a backseat to other drug problems.

In comparing the information provided by county sheriffs with that from state and federal law enforcement, it appeared that local authorities were far more knowledgeable about the individuals involved in growing. Having spent most of their lives in the area and personally knowing many of the county's residents, they often had a much richer understanding of the individuals involved. In contrast, state officials were more knowledgeable about patterns and trends in growing because they handled cases in several counties.

During the 1980s there was a shift away from local enforcement of marijuana toward state and federal enforcement. When initially contacted by mail, several sheriffs indicated they automatically referred all such cases to the state police. Others have shifted more cases to the state police, particularly if a case appears large and may have complicated forfeiture issues. There were two reasons for this shift. First, the budgets of many sheriffs' departments saw little growth during the 1980s, while expenses continued to rise. Making arrests in domestic cultivation cases, as opposed to simply eradicating plants, is very labor-intensive, often requiring "sitting on" a field for several weeks. The costs of these operations quickly accumulate, and sheriffs' departments lack the manpower to do this work. One sheriff reported eradicating fifteen to twenty plots of marijuana each year. When asked how many arrests were made in a typical year, he responded, "None." In fact, only one arrest for growing had been made in a six-year period. His department was so short-handed that he himself had to work an eight-hour patrol shift to cover basic patrol functions of the department. While equipment, such as helicopters, airplanes, and special cameras, was appreciated by these officers, most expressed a more pressing need for manpower.

P22:   Well, we don't have the proper equipment to stake out a large marijuana field. What you need is time-lapse cameras. You need sensor devices if you want to catch them in the act of harvesting. Or you have to put somebody over there, camping out twenty-four hours a day hoping to catch them. It's really difficult for us to justify spending a lot of money, putting somebody out there to camp twenty-four hours a day for maybe 30–60–90 days.

P26:   They can give me all the equipment in the world, but if I haven't got the manpower to utilize that equipment, it sits down in my storeroom and doesn't get used.

P18:   I served on a commission. There were twenty-two people on this commission and it was aimed at the production of marijuana. I brought it up that we needed more conservation officers in this area, not only for marijuana but for deer poaching, because we have so many deer. There was no one on that commission but myself who was from southern Illinois. Everybody else was from Chicago and places far away. Their immediate solution was to buy two airplanes. I just sat there and laughed at them. You know, when you fly over my county what you see are the tops of about ten million trees. You cannot find marijuana from the air in my county. They couldn't understand that, so I resigned. What they needed was more people on the ground. You have to have more people on the ground, that's all there is to it.

Given these restrictions, it was surprising to find several sheriffs who simply made time to stake out fields, often by doing without sleep and working back-to-back shifts.

P09:   I've only got three deputies, which is more than I used to have. Even the four of us, having to be around seven days a week twenty-four hours a day, is just not enough if you do anything extra rather than just your work. But we have set on places as long as two or three weeks. To me, pulling the

plants is the last resort. Now, if I find plants that haven't
been taken care of, I would pull those. But if I find a good
patch that's being cultivated, I'll sit on that.

A second reason for the shift from local to state enforcement of
marijuana laws, itself related to shrinking budgets, was the rise of task forces
and multicounty enforcement groups that allowed several agencies to pool
resources while also sharing the benefits, such as income from forfeiture.
It appears that enforcement efforts suffer considerably when local
authorities are not involved. While they lack the manpower and technology of
the state or federal police, their knowledge of the terrain and the local people
is very important. One sheriff, whose office was chronically understaffed, was
asked about utilizing the DEA to assist in marijuana raids.

P18:   I did call the feds in a couple of times. Then I quit. I have
        no confidence in them. In the first place, they are ego-
        maniacs. They think they are really something on a stick.
        They come into an area like this, of which they know nothing.
        They don't know the history of it, the people, the terrain.
        They can mess up an investigation faster than you can shake
        a stick at it. I had two unfortunate experiences. One was
        with this two-and-a-half-million-dollar patch we had. I could
        see it was quite an important thing; I mean we really needed
        to catch somebody. So I called in the DEA. You would have
        thought they were a SWAT team. They came in with all this
        fancy stuff. You can't imagine the equipment and stuff they
        had with them. I'm sure, just by the way they approached the
        plot, they scared the people off. [He said that by their
        approach the growers probably saw them well before they
        arrived at the patch.] And eventually, all we did was pull all
        the plants and burn them. I decided after that we would
        handle it ourselves, because we knew more about the territory
        than any of them did.

This concern about where resources should be placed has also been
voiced by local sheriffs elsewhere. In California, for example, a contingent of
200 army soldiers, national guardsmen, and federal agents spent two weeks
clearing out growing operations in the King Range National Conservation Area
in northern California. As a result of their efforts, 1,200 plants were destroyed,
but not everyone was satisfied.

        "This is so frustrating when the Federal Government comes in
        and spends enough money that would keep my operation
        going for three or four years," said Sheriff David Renner of

> Humboldt County. His team of five deputies, cooperating with the state's seven-year-old Campaign Against Marijuana Planting, destroyed over 3,000 plants in one day this week.
>
> "If the Feds have the money for this kind of operation," Sheriff Renner said, "they ought to give it to local law enforcement that is more effective and is truly responsible to local citizens. Their results speak for themselves and they are not good." (Bishop, 1990)

In Illinois, there were only a few complaints from sheriffs about the state police, and these focused on the flow of information about drug investigations. Several sheriffs complained that while they were expected to give all of their information to the ISP, the state police did not always reciprocate. One sheriff discussed raids by the state police, who were heavily armed and in camouflage. He had not been told in advance of these raids and was concerned that such a lack of coordination could easily lead to accidents in which local police mistook the state police for dangerous people and fired upon them.

In several districts the state police have worked hard to cultivate good relations with local authorities. The development of task forces involving several counties and the state police also appears useful as a way to combine the resources of state and federal authorities with the knowledge of local police. Overall, the relationships between state and local authorities seem to have improved during the 1980s.

Interviewing both state and local authorities allowed the comments of growers to be juxtaposed against those of law enforcement, with the understanding that each group is hardly neutral on the subject. As noted above, the interviews with authorities were relatively unstructured. Consequently, included below are only those subject areas that generated the most discussion or about which authorities were most informed.

WHO GROWS AND WHY

Police shared the growers' assessment that entering the marijuana business was easy, particularly obtaining seeds and getting started. The risks began when growers tried to sell their product or when their operations became relatively large.

Police saw a range of people entering the marijuana business, although they emphasized the use of marijuana and other drugs by growers as a motivating factor. They also placed a heavy emphasis on the money from growing, reiterating the greed and self-serving nature of growers. Several explicitly divided growers into two categories, those whose involvement was tied to drug use and those whose motivation was primarily to make money.

P06:   I would say probably half of the growers are from that
        generation that thinks there's nothing wrong with it, never will
        be anything wrong with it, still think it ought to be legalized,
        and "By God, I can do it." And the other half says, "No, it's
        wrong, we know that, but it's a business, nothing personal, it's
        a business."

P11:   There are two reasons why people manufacture or cultivate it.
        One is for their own personal use. The other is for the
        money—the high profit. A lot of your small-time growers do
        it basically for their own personal use or for the use of their
        friends. They'll probably sell, but sell in small quantities to
        personal friends of theirs. I think there is a distinct difference
        when you get into a large quantity, because then it's going to
        be the financial reward.

REWARDS OF GROWING

        Growers emphasized the rewards of growing that went beyond simple
money. Police gave a greater emphasis to the money as a motivating factor,
but several also noted the issue of pride.

P02:   This guy was really proud; I'll never forget him. When I was
        on the stand, at his preliminary hearing, he acted as his own
        defense attorney and he asked me, "Detective X, in all your
        years of being a detective, have you worked a lot of marijuana
        cases?" I said, "Yes." He said, "Would you say that these
        plants from some of my crop are the best plants that you've
        ever seen?" I said, "Yes." He said, "Thank you, no further
        questions."

P06:   They're very proud of their accomplishments, and it's just like
        showing a prize cow at the county fair. "Hey, look at this
        baby. I've got the mother plant here." I had one guy who
        called it "Mom." That was his mother plant, he made clip-
        pings from that, and was very proud of that. I can't explain
        it any better than to say it's the pride of accomplishment. I
        wish I could channel some of their efforts elsewhere.

P11:   I think it's just like in agriculture; they're pleased with how
        much they can produce and in the quality of the marijuana.
        X is a classic example of that. He's out there every day
        rubbing, touching, smelling, opening them up. It's just like a

person who brings big tomatoes in and shows everybody, "Look what I grew." You can't do that with marijuana, but when it hits the market, people are going to know it and the users are going to talk, "Hey, it's good shit, we want some more of this."

P15:   Most of them around here seem to start growing for either themselves or close friends, so they want to do the best they can, and when they get together, it seems like they just keep improving to the point of becoming professional gardeners, almost.

Of course, law-enforcement officers are somewhat shielded from this type of information because of their roles. One officer spoke about this lack of communication.

P22:   Well, we're the bad guys who arrest them, and they're not prone to talk to us, to brag about what they've got. Very rarely do we get to sit down and talk to one of these guys, slap them on the back, and say, "Gee, that's some marijuana."

RISK FROM GROWING

Both growers and authorities saw the risk of arrest as small. For both groups the estimated likelihood of arrest ranged from no chance to almost certainty, but overall they guessed about 25 percent were caught. The primary difference was that authorities saw the risk as small *in any given year*, believing that over time the small annual risk accumulated and that eventually nearly all growers would be caught.

When officials were asked the longest period of time someone had been growing marijuana before being caught, their estimates were similar to those given by growers who were asked the same question. Most said two or three years, with a few knowing of growers who had been involved for as long as ten or twenty years.

VIOLENCE AND GROWING

Growers painted a picture of their activities as essentially nonviolent, but some might argue this characterization is hardly from a neutral source and that it is in the growers' self-interest to describe themselves in this way. In contrast, it might be expected that the interests of law-enforcement officers would be in highlighting violence, so as to make it clear that the activities of these growers are anything but harmless. Thus, discussion of violence by officials was particularly important for this study. The reports of law enforcement on violence by marijuana growers in Illinois generally confirmed the images presented by growers. Instances of violence were rarely reported by officials.

Q: Have you had any problems with violence from growers, booby traps or anything like that?

P02:   Once we thought we were going to run into trip wires, and we thought it included traps. It turned out it was just to hold the plants up.

P09:   Not around here, no.

P10:   No, that's one thing we've been very lucky on. We have heavy shoes, that's about the only protection we use from it. You know, in case we step on something. We haven't had any booby traps.

P15:   No, a few rumors, but nothing that we've uncovered or seen.

P16:   No. Every time we have anticipated a violent-type situation, we have used a tactical team to go in and neutralize the site, and we've never come across any traps.

P26:   No . . . basically we're still not violent up here. We're getting worse, it seems like every time we do a search warrant, we're getting guns, but we haven't had any booby trapping of the fields—we haven't had any real violence connected with anything. And, usually when we hit a place and we get the person who is growing, he is for the most part nonviolent and in the surprise of us being there we don't have any problem.

On the issue of violence an interesting pattern emerged. While violence was not reported by these officials and such things as booby traps were rarely found, several officials believed violence was common in other sections of the state and that they had simply been lucky. However, when interviews were conducted in other parts of the state, no instances of violence could be found. One official said, for example, there were no instances of violence in his jurisdiction but described the Shawnee National Forest as a DMZ. Interviews with a representative of the Shawnee National Forest and with several sheriffs near the forest indicated no problems with violence there, but they believed it was a problem in other parts of the state.   Another sheriff reported the following:

P11:   No, but Sheriff X, when I was talking to him at a conference,
          said that two of the fields they've already entered this year
          had booby traps and different devices. They don't really feel
          they were put there for law enforcement; they think they were
          there for the competition, but it's always possible.

When later interviewed, Sheriff X was asked about violence and reported there had been no trouble with violence of any kind from growers. He said he had heard about it in other places but had never experienced it in his county. He had come across a patch with a trip wire hooked up, but whatever was going to be put on the other end was never connected.

Thus, violence in the marijuana fields seems to have become something of a legend or folk tale among law-enforcement officers in Illinois. The few officials who did indicate violence associated with growing in their jurisdictions could not give specific examples.

The fact that violence is a continued concern among officials despite the absence of violence by growers does not mean their concern is unjustified. It would take only one violent grower to make the precautions of officials worth the time and effort. It is clearly safer for them to err on the side of precaution. Also, while violent people have not been drawn to marijuana growing in Illinois, there is no reason why they cannot enter the business at any time.

CHANGING GROWING TECHNIQUES

There was general agreement by officials that during the 1980s the techniques used by commercial growers had been changing. Outdoor crops were less frequently planted in large single plots but were spread out in smaller clusters and were planted in irregular patterns, which took advantage of natural vegetation for cover. Officials reported an increase in indoor growing and in the sophistication of indoor operations. All of these trends were expected to continue into the 1990s.

OTHER DRUGS

Officials were divided over the issue of whether marijuana growers become involved in the use of other drugs or in other aspects of the drug business. Some officials were quick to link marijuana with the use of other drugs, and several saw marijuana growing as a way to support a cocaine habit.

P06:   From experience, I've seen where they have been involved in marijuana, then they might come up with a cocaine habit, and because they are using cocaine for themselves, they have to buy cocaine. So they're not in the cocaine distribution system, . . . Marijuana is still their cash flow base, with their income coming from marijuana, so they can turn around and buy cocaine.

P07:   It has been our experience from investigations, interviews, and prosecutions that people who are in the home-grown sin-semilla operations inevitably are branching out into cocaine. The reason for this is that marijuana is an inexpensive crop to produce. Then they can take the proceeds, reinvest it in cocaine, and make additional monies.

P08:   It seems like marijuana and cocaine go hand in hand for some reason; I think that went back to the Colombian pot days. But there are a lot of people who just strictly stay with marijuana.

Other officials made a distinction between marijuana growers and those in the business of cocaine or heroin.

P11:   No. I really don't believe that [growers become involved with other drugs]. I believe your marijuana growers are probably going to stick to marijuana. . . . I don't know if they are a different type of person, but it takes a person who is pretty involved in horticulture and stuff like that to get involved in growing. After you specialize in a field like that, why transfer yourself to some chemical-type field?

P24:   I don't feel the ones who are growing marijuana are involved in any of the other drugs. We had one fellow who grew fields away from here. We caught him with a bunch of it in his car and then later there was a much bigger investigation because he was growing fields of it in Iowa. But, interestingly enough, he hated the cocaine dealers. He just despised cocaine, and yet his marijuana was fine.

P07:   Historically, marijuana dealers are less prone to violence than your cocaine individuals. In our major conspiracies involving large-scale marijuana importation and distribution, there have been occasions of violence, homicides, but when you get over into the cocaine side of it, the propensity for violence is so much greater.

P30:   It seems like they [marijuana growers] are a different group, totally different. People in marijuana growing started out because they used marijuana on regular occasions. . . . You know, if you wanted to look across the United States, there are probably not too many pro-marijuana groups that would say LSD and cocaine and heroin are not harmful to you.

P15:   What really surprised me was that this grower said he was going to pull his kids out of the local schools because of the crack and cocaine in them, but the marijuana didn't bother him. He just said, "I can't see putting my kids in that school where all that cocaine is."

LEGALIZING MARIJUANA

It should not be surprising that officials who emphasize marijuana enforcement oppose legalizing marijuana. What was surprising was that officials and growers shared a concern about marijuana being available to young people. Growers either opposed legalization or favored legal access for adults only. Police not only saw it as harmful to adults but believed that under any legalization scheme young people would have greater access to marijuana. A few thought legalization for adults only might happen in the future, but they were not enthused about the prospect.

EFFECTS ON THE COMMUNITY

Officers were also asked about the effects of marijuana growing on the local community. Officers were divided on this issue, some believed it had almost no impact on the community while others believed that marijuana growing was directly tied to other forms of crime. More common, however, was a middle position in which officials did not see the growers themselves as a problem but felt their activities set the stage for trouble. This trouble included increased local drug use, potential violence from and against marijuana thieves, and the likelihood that marijuana production would bring criminal types into the community to purchase or distribute the product.

Despite the potentially large profits that can be made by growing marijuana, officials doubted the marijuana industry had much financial impact on their local communities. Those who sold to local users were basically keeping money in the area and those who sold larger amounts may have brought in money from the outside, but the money involved was insignificant compared with legitimate sources. In interviews with both growers and officials there were few mentions of local businesses whose livelihood depended on the marijuana industry.

Finally, several were concerned about the impact of marijuana growers on the public's feelings of safety.

P15:   It gave a lot of people who moved to our county from another area a feeling that "I'm away from the big city, I'm away from marijuana and drugs, and here it is, right in my back yard." I think it really has an impact on people like that coming out here to get away from it all, to settle down in a quiet place.

P11:   I don't really think it's a bad reflection on the community itself. I just think that sometimes it alerts the community that "My God, this stuff is going on right here." I really don't think it has any other harmful effects on the community.

People living in rural areas sometimes have a stereotypical image of the drug problem as primarily an urban problem, and the arrest of a local marijuana grower challenges this stereotype.

CHANGES IN THE LAW

It might be expected that police feel "handcuffed" by rules of criminal procedure and that most would recommend easing procedural protections for defendants as a way to make their job easier. In fact, none of the officers involved complained about procedural restrictions, although several would have liked harsher penalties.

Q: Are there changes you would like to see in the law to make your job easier?
P11:   Oh, I don't think our job is ever going to get easier. I think the laws we have to work under are very fair, for not only law enforcement but also for the protection of citizen's rights. I think you have to have certain rules and regulations to protect the private citizens who are not involved.

P08:   I think the laws are adequate to be honest with you. Unfortunately, you've got state's attorneys who choose to plea-bargain cases, and you've got judges who are very lenient on drug offenders in certain cases.

P09:   No, I don't think so. Naturally, I'd like to see them do away
        with Miranda, but you've got to have that balance. People
        have their rights even though they're crooks, and I can live
        with that.

P18:   The only thing I would like to see is for the courts to hit them
        a little harder. It is always a little irritating to me to spend
        hours and hours and hours looking for the stuff. You get into
        court and they more or less, too often, slap them on the wrist.
        You have to be tough or it won't make an impression on
        them.

A more common complaint, particularly among sheriffs, was a lack of
funding for manpower to locate and stake out fields. In addition, several would
have preferred to see state forfeiture procedures simplified, something that was
done by the state legislature in the fall of 1990.

P22:   We have pretty good laws. What would make our job easier
        would be changes in our budget system. We need more
        liberalized ways to get money. We just don't have the assets
        to do it [wipe out drugs].

At the same time they argued for more resources, nearly all were
pessimistic about the willingness of the public to increase taxes to fund further
marijuana eradication efforts. They were also very skeptical about the ability
of the police to stop marijuana growing even if they had all the resources they
needed.

P11:   No. That would be like saying you could completely stop
        crime if you had enough police, and I don't think a society can
        exist without the criminal element.

P22:   You'd have to get access to every piece of land in every
        county in Illinois.

P18:   No. They could make a bigger dent in it, but they could
        never stop it.

P12:   Absolutely not.

VARIATIONS AMONG STATES

This study focused on growers in Illinois, but it will be more useful if it illustrates how the patterns in Illinois fit the country as a whole. During the study, news reports and personal communications about marijuana growers in Kentucky suggested that growing conditions there might be different. It became increasingly clear that to understand the Illinois data, comparisons with other states would be necessary, even if such comparisons had to be preliminary.

It was beyond the scope of the study to duplicate this work in other states, but it was possible to interview a few officials from surrounding states and to compare their descriptions of growing with those from Illinois. Thirteen officials were interviewed, including five from Kentucky, five from Indiana, and one each from Missouri, Tennessee, and Hawaii. Interviews were with state police, DEA, sheriffs, and a representative of a national forest. These six states (including Illinois) are a good group to include in this study. Five of these states were among the top ten states for marijuana seizures in 1990 and the sixth state (Indiana) ranked twelfth among states (DEA, 1990).

In addition, interviews were supplemented with newspaper accounts of growing in these states, although the process of locating these accounts was neither systematic nor thorough. The labor-intensive process required to locate Illinois cases precluded using the same procedures in these other states. Thus growers and officials could not be used to confirm patterns reported by each other. Earlier chapters were designed to inform readers about particular patterns. This chapter is intended merely to suggest interstate patterns that are relevant for policy and that merit verification through more systematic study.

In each case, marijuana cultivation was reported throughout much of the state but was more frequent in one region. In Illinois, Indiana, and Missouri more marijuana was cultivated in the south. In Kentucky and Tennessee more growing occurred on the eastern side of the state. In Hawaii the greatest problem was on the main island of Hawaii.

These growing regions were not only distinctive because of marijuana but were culturally and economically different from the rest of the state. Growing was more common in counties with less economic development and where government rules and regulations were less strict. Although this was not measured, it appeared that counties in which growing was most prevalent were also those most resistant to such government regulations as zoning.

Only in Kentucky were there counties in which the local economy would be completely wiped out if marijuana production ended. In Tennessee there were several counties in which the sudden end of marijuana production would have a substantial impact on the local economy. In the remaining states the economic impact of marijuana growing was believed to be less profound.

The officers who participated in the study were aware that the rural setting shaped both the nature of crime and their response to it. However, those who were raised in rural areas seemed to most appreciate this distinction and to best utilize it in their police work.

P14:   You can't act overly high and mighty with them, you won't get any cooperation. In the big cities, that's what you do, you come on strong, "I'm the boss." That's often a very effective method there, but not out here in the rural areas. . . . This summer I went down and there was a guy with maybe 200 plants spread out over a small farm. I was fairly confident it was there and I pull up in his driveway. He was unloading wood, I'm in the pickup truck, and obviously he knows who I am. I walked up and told him what I was doing there. I said, "I've come to get your marijuana and we're going to be doing an open field search. We're not going to be going through your barns or anything right now. You've got some marijuana out there and I've just come up here to tell you what I'm doing." I helped him unload his wood and then I said, "I'm going down by the pond and look at this marijuana. I'll be back in a minute." I went down, looked at it, and came back up. I said, "Well, your marijuana is down there," and then I went ahead and helped him unload some more wood and talked about it. He went to jail with no problem. I think this was the kind of guy who would have liked to have fought you. But because of the way I handled it, he wasn't going to fight anybody. Because I didn't go in there and say, "You're a marijuana grower and you're worthless." A lot of times if you're dealing with people in these rural areas, they don't have a problem with you coming in and arresting them. They just want to be treated like human beings.

In 1990 no wild marijuana was found in Tennessee and Hawaii. Kentucky, Indiana, and Missouri had wild marijuana, and in each case the prime counties for cultivated marijuana were not usually those where the most ditchweed was eradicated. This, too, was partly related to economics. During the war hemp was planted on the richest farmland, and thus in areas of relative economic prosperity. Contemporary marijuana cultivators were more often in economically depressed rural areas in which the land was not well suited for the large-scale cultivation of traditional crops.

In Kentucky, Indiana, Missouri, and Tennessee there was an absence of minority growers, although each state had rural counties with substantial minority populations. In each of these states most growers were middle-aged, or older, white males. Women were infrequently involved as sole growers but sometimes provided assistance to male companions.

States differed in the violence associated with growing.   Illinois reported almost no violence.   Indiana, Tennessee, Hawaii, and Missouri reported some booby traps, although these were usually nonlethal warning devices designed to frighten intruders.   In Tennessee, for example, there were some passive nonlethal devices—fishhooks suspended across a path, spikes in the ground pointing upward, and so on.   There were also reports of "false booby traps," such as signs warning of traps where none existed.   More violence was reported in Kentucky, but it was difficult to separate violence that was the product of the marijuana industry from that endemic to the local area.   Some ancillary crime was associated with marijuana production in each state.   In Kentucky and Tennessee some growers had long family histories of criminal activities (e.g., moonshining, dealing in stolen auto parts, vice), and marijuana was simply the most recent area into which they had ventured.

The DEA's annual report on marijuana eradication lists the number of arrests and the number of weapons seized for each state (DEA, 1990). Nationally, in 1990 the DEA reported 5,729 marijuana arrests and the seizure of 3,210 weapons—about one weapon for every two arrests.   Kentucky and Missouri reflected this 1:2 ratio, but the remaining states had fewer weapons per arrest than the national average.   In Hawaii, for example, there was only one weapon seized for every twenty-two arrests.   This may reflect the fact that guns are a measure of violence that is too narrow.   In rural areas the presence of guns per se may say little about the potential for violence (see chapter 6), which might be expressed in other ways.   Kentucky, for example, was reportedly among the leading states in the theft of dynamite, which is extensively used in coal mining.   Officials there were always alert to the possibility that marijuana fields were rigged with explosive devices.

Aside from Kentucky, most growing appears to have no direct link to organized networks of growers.   Although they were loosely structured, Kentucky's "cornbread mafia" had operations in Illinois, Indiana, Missouri, and a number of other midwestern states.   No comparable groups have yet been found that originate in Illinois, Indiana, Missouri, or Hawaii, although a few small networks were reported.   This may change over time, since there is nothing about marijuana growing that precludes cooperatives from forming in these states.

Another indicator of the relative extent of the problem is the existence of defense attorneys with a reputation for defending marijuana growers. Of course, attorneys who focus on drug cases are common, but those versed in marijuana cultivation cases are not.   There were reports of these attorneys in Missouri and Kentucky, but no such legal specialists were reported in Illinois, Indiana, Tennessee, or Hawaii.

Missouri and Kentucky shared another indicator of sophistication among growers in their dealings with the law.   In both states there were reports of "decoy plots," used by growers to divert police and thieves from their main plots.   These decoy plots were likely to be found but could not be tied to the grower. The police used valuable time and the greed of thieves was partially satiated.

P23:   Last year there were what I call "gimme plots." They would put a small group of marijuana in a very obvious location on a trail and then actually have their main body of plants down some place beyond that, or off to the side, so that if law enforcement or a raider or a pirate would come in he'd find this first little plot and take it off figuring he had the plot.

In Illinois, Indiana, and Missouri local sheriffs were generally very cooperative in marijuana eradication and often took the initiative on marijuana cultivation cases. These actions by sheriffs had strong public support and were the kinds of activities that would help their reelection. Tennessee reported a few corrupt (or at least tolerant) sheriffs in the most economically depressed and least-populated counties.

In eastern Kentucky, local sheriffs played a relatively minor role in local law enforcement of any kind and steered a wide path from marijuana enforcement. Most limited their official activities to tax collection. There was sufficient public support for marijuana growing that sheriffs in eastern Kentucky who became actively involved in marijuana enforcement could risk defeat in the next election. This was particularly important in counties where unemployment was high and elected positions, such as sheriff, were prized for providing a stable and relatively good income. In these counties sheriffs who were voted out of office could not always count on having another source of income. At the time of the interviews there were rumors of marijuana-related corruption among local authorities in Kentucky, and several months after the interviews four county sheriffs, a sheriff's deputy, and a local police chief were arrested and charged with conspiracy to extort money and protect drug shipments in eastern Kentucky. Their activities permitted, not only the production of local marijuana, but the transshipment of cocaine through their county ("Six Kentucky Law Officers Arrested on Drug Charges," 1990). No comparable levels of corruption were reported for Illinois, Indiana, or Missouri, although some problems were reported in Tennessee.

Public support for growing was strongest in eastern Kentucky, where state police were refused food and gasoline in marijuana-producing counties, and their families were made to feel unwelcome. For example, a state trooper's wife was reportedly approached after church by a local woman who asked, "Why does your husband want to take Christmas away from our children?" In one Kentucky county, a story in *USA Today* (Kelly, 1989) reported that as many as 40 percent of the citizens were involved in marijuana growing. Nothing comparable to this was found in Illinois or reported for Indiana. One state police officer was very much offended by a suggestion that citizens might be somewhat tolerant of growers. Other interviews suggested his indignation was justified. There were areas of Missouri where editorials supporting legalization and criticizing eradication efforts were published in local newspapers, but the level of tolerance for growers did not approach that reported for eastern Kentucky.

In Illinois, Missouri, and Hawaii the majority of marijuana growers began as users, and officials believed they commonly experimented with other drugs. In Indiana and Tennessee most growers were users, but there were more reports of arrested growers emphatically denying the use of any drugs. In Kentucky abstinence from marijuana and other drugs seemed more common than in the other states. One large-scale Kentucky grower did not use tobacco, alcohol, or other drugs and was a leader in his local church. However, this was probably not a typical case. Growers in Kentucky were still more likely than not to use marijuana, and some officials believed that for several marijuana growing supported a cocaine habit.

Secrecy among growers was a common theme across these states. Kentucky again stands in contrast, however. The level of secrecy among growers in Kentucky was particularly strong in dealings with people outside of the local community. For example, at the time officials were interviewed, there had been indictments against seventy people linked to the cornbread mafia. Although they were facing fifteen to twenty years in prison, *none* had been willing to provide the names of others connected to the organization. An official from another state commented on this reticence.

P31:   People in rural areas tend to be pretty conservative generally and don't want government coming in, or an outsider coming in, or foreigners coming in. They want the status quo and that's it. And when they develop a cancer from within, they don't want it going out. They don't want people telling about it and they don't want people rocking the boat. They are the same people who will ostracize members of their society who get caught doing this [marijuana growing].

Variations in marijuana-growing patterns and in the characteristics of marijuana growers between and within states comprise an area that needs further study. Understanding why these variations are so striking may prove valuable in understanding why domestic cultivation is more common in some areas than in others. Growers in Kentucky have probably received most attention in the national press, and the nature of the problem there merits concern. It is clear that Kentucky is atypical and in a number of ways is a caricature of the problem, in which essential features of growing and growers are exaggerated.

SUMMARY

As might be expected, law-enforcement officers charged with marijuana eradication took a more critical view of growers than did the growers themselves. Officers were more likely to emphasize the use of other drugs by marijuana growers and the role of growing in local crime.

What was interesting was the number of issues on which they were in basic agreement: the lack of violence among these growers, an expressed concern about marijuana use by young people, the ease of getting into the marijuana business, and the low risk facing most growers in any given year. Given that growers and the police approach the issue from two entirely different world views, it was surprising there were any areas of basic agreement.

As a group these officers were satisfied with the procedural rules of law that made their job more difficult but also protected the rights of citizens. Given the choice, they would prefer harsher sentences or at least the more strict application of penalties already in law. They would have preferred simpler state-level procedures for forfeiture (something the Illinois legislature did shortly after the interviews). They realized that citizens would probably not support tax increases to fund more intensive marijuana eradication efforts, and they did not think the problem could be solved only by increasing enforcement efforts. Yet they did feel the need for larger budgets that would include lines for additional personnel.

In addition to Illinois, officials from five states were interviewed about marijuana production. These interviews suggested patterns common to these states. Growing tended to be more concentrated in those rural areas that were less economically prosperous. In most states violence was not a typical feature of marijuana growing and secrecy among growers was a common theme. Perhaps more important were the observed differences among these states. There was considerable variation in public support for growers, the sophistication of growing operations, the corruption of local officials, and the existence of wild marijuana. The significance of these interstate variations is among the subjects of the next chapter, which outlines some of the policy implications of this research.

10

POLICY IMPLICATIONS

The purpose of this study was to describe the kinds of people involved in the domestic marijuana industry and the factors that motivated them. As such, the information presented here goes well beyond that which can be garnered from simple police reports, although official data on patterns of arrest were utilized to supplement interview data.

This was not designed as a policy study. The drug area is replete with well-intentioned policies, which, in hindsight, create problems of their own (Weisheit, in press). This tendency was seen in the rise of the domestic marijuana industry, which was probably hastened by official policies toward marijuana importation. Rather than outlining specific policies, this discussion highlights findings that may have implications for the policy process.

These observations are made with several caveats in mind. First, the focus is not on casual marijuana use or the cultivation of a few plants for personal consumption, but on commercial marijuana growers. Second, it is presumed that legalization is not a realistic prospect at this time, and this is particularly true of commercial marijuana cultivation. A society that places increasing legal and administrative restrictions on the use of tobacco seems unlikely to favor legalizing commercial marijuana cultivation. Finally, it is presumed that even those who favor legalizing marijuana should be concerned about the future direction of the domestic industry and should support policies designed to minimize violence and the involvement of organized crime. With these caveats in mind, the following factors should be considered in the development of policies to restrict commercial marijuana cultivation.

Economic Considerations. The problem of domestic marijuana cultivation is fundamentally an economic problem. Official policies that focus on forfeiture and the seizure of assets have had an impact on large-scale growers and have proved a boon to law-enforcement agencies. These policies, however, have the greatest impact on growers who plan to become wealthy from their activities and probably have minimal impact on those who begin growing precisely *because* they have few resources. Such policies are also more reactive than proactive. Their utility for prevention is less clear, although they may serve a preventative function when applied to *suppliers* of growing equipment and materials.

For those driven to growing by economic necessity, programs designed to provide alternative employment might be valuable supplements to existing policies. There is talk, for example, of building a U.S. penitentiary in one of the Kentucky counties most noted for marijuana growing. It is also a county in which nearly half of the people have legitimate incomes below the poverty level. It will be interesting to see how the availability of alternative employment opportunities changes public attitudes toward growing in that county.

Other Rewards from Growing. While many enter the marijuana business for economic reasons, it is important to recognize that for a substantial proportion of growers there are rewards that go beyond cash. These people are likely to continue growing even if they stop selling their crop to others. For these growers the issue is not developing alternative income sources, but finding alternative outlets for their fascination with growing—or at least moving them out of commercial production.

Changes in Growing Techniques. Both growers and police reported a shift toward indoor growing. This has several implications for the nature of the marijuana problem. First, it obviously creates a year-round growing season. Second, because it requires more capital (for equipment, supplies, and utilities), there are more incentives for growers to work together and form organizations. Third, the increased expense of growing each plant and space limitations encourage indoor growers to develop more potent strains. Fourth, the increased capital expenditures along with the fact that indoor growing is more easily tied to individuals (i.e., an arrest will likely follow the detection of an indoor operation) may encourage growers to increase defensive measures, including the use of booby traps and weapons. Finally, indoor growing makes it possible to move domestic marijuana cultivation from rural to urban areas. Several growers and police officials reported they expected to see urban warehouse operations within a few years.

Community Support. Any policies that hope to curtail domestic marijuana cultivation must take into account the rural setting in which growing takes place and the importance of community in that setting. As the experiences in Kentucky show, eradicating marijuana without community support is extremely difficult. In other states community support exists but is under-utilized. One Illinois county had a program to train farmers to recognize marijuana plants, but there were few programs that utilized hunters, utility workers, or amateur pilots.

Local versus State or Federal Efforts: It is important that local officials play a role in the investigation of crimes, such as marijuana cultivation, in rural areas. Their knowledge of the terrain and the people is an extremely valuable resource that should be emphasized. Developing a policy that addresses this consideration is complicated by corruption of local officials. This is not a problem in most jurisdictions, but Kentucky again illustrates a worst-case scenario around which policies must be constructed.

In contrast, the strength of state and federal officers is in their ability to see the "big picture" and to have more resources at their disposal. The best policies would seem to be those in which local knowledge is combined with state and federal resources, and in which local authorities have some role in directing activities. In particular, manpower for local agencies was frequently cited as a pressing need.

Interstate Variations. There are clear interstate and intrastate variations in the nature of the marijuana industry and these variations are very much the product of climate, economics, and local culture. These differences suggest it would be wrong to develop a single national strategy for eradicating cultivated marijuana unless that policy is flexible enough to take these local variations into account.

Organized Marijuana Growing. Outside of Kentucky the areas included in this study showed little evidence that growers operate within even loosely structured cooperative organizations. The more common circumstance is the independent entrepreneur who is linked to several buyers but is not directly part of a larger enterprise. Where networks of growers exist, these are more likely to be based on friendship than on business.

Secrecy and Marijuana Growing. Secrecy is a common feature of marijuana growing and people in the rural areas in which it occurs often show a strong distrust of outsiders. These facts do not bode well for outside investigators and again suggest the value of investigations directed by local officials familiar with the people, the terrain, and the culture.

Marijuana and Other Drugs. Those who grow marijuana often use it and often experiment with other drugs. The networks by which they market their marijuana, however, are generally not structured to encourage dealing in other drugs. That is, marijuana production does not seem to serve as a "gateway" to involvement in the distribution of other drugs. Marijuana growers may use their profits to buy cocaine, for example. And they may enter the cocaine distribution market, but this is not because they are in the marijuana market. Those who deal in marijuana do not have automatic access to the cocaine distribution market. Most commercial marijuana growers probably have little interest in entering other drug markets. Many growers make a sharp distinction between their activities and dealing in other drugs. Further, simply dealing other drugs does not provide the kinds of intangible rewards that accompany marijuana growing.

Policies that equate marijuana with other drugs only encourage growers and users to minimize the distinction. It makes it easier for them to rationalize involvement with other drugs and probably does nothing to keep them from marijuana.

Violence in the Marijuana Industry. Fortunately, the marijuana industry has little of the violence associated with cocaine distribution or with street-level heroin dealing. Policies designed to reduce production should be carefully framed so that violent people are not encouraged to enter the business and drive out nonviolent people. When dealing with rural offenders, prosecutors and judges, particularly those from the federal system who may be unfamiliar with the local area, should be sensitive to the very different meaning firearms have in rural culture.

SUMMARY

There are important differences between marijuana cultivation and urban drug problems that suggest that drug policies regarding domestic cultivation cannot simply be transplanted versions of urban models for responding to drug problems. These differences include features of the rural setting, distinctive characteristics of marijuana growers, the lower level of violence, and the distinction made by both growers and users between marijuana and "hard" drugs. The extent to which growing is lucrative suggests the importance of economic considerations, but the intangible rewards of growing must also be taken into account when setting policy. Further, marijuana growing is distinct from other drug-trafficking activities in that it is land-bound and labor-intensive. Requiring a commitment of time, labor, and resources means that people are less free to drift in and out of marijuana cultivation than is true for other types of drug work.

Appendix A

RESEARCH DESIGN
AND PLAN

There was too little knowledge about marijuana growers at the start of the study to use such tools of traditional quantitative research as the experimental design or the epidemiological study. Out of necessity the study focused on etiology using qualitative research techniques, though whenever possible, quantitative techniques were also incorporated. For example, available literature was used to develop a typology of growers, put forth tentative hypotheses, and outline research questions. While these preliminary ideas served as starting points, it was understood from the beginning that the issues and questions might change as the study progressed.

IDENTIFYING CASES

The first task was to identify cases in Illinois in which someone had been arrested for growing marijuana for profit. The researcher initially had information about five such cases. To find more cases, letters were sent to three people in each Illinois county (except for Cook County, which is entirely urban): the county sheriff, the editor of the major county newspaper, and the county extension agent. The letters explained the project and mentioned that a staff member would be calling for information. When calling, it quickly became clear that county extension agents were not a good source for this type of information. They either took no notice of such cases or chose not to talk about them. Subsequent calls focused on sheriffs and newspaper editors. A month later, similar letters and follow-up calls were directed to state's attorneys.

As cases were identified, it was decided that a working definition of a commercial grower would include all marijuana growing cases involving twenty or more plants for which a formal arrest had been made. A cutoff of twenty plants was chosen so it was likely the growing was for profit. Not everyone who grows twenty plants will necessarily be growing for profit—some may be users who simply give away surpluses. Similarly, some growers with fewer than twenty plants are growing strictly for profit. In addition, relying only on numbers ignores the fact that plants vary in size and weight, depending on when in the growing season they are seized. In one case a person was arrested for growing twenty-eight plants. The plants had only recently sprouted and combined weighed only 22.5 grams (less than an ounce). Despite these qualifications, twenty plants seemed a reasonable cutoff to eliminate cases in which growing was for personal use rather than profit.

To obtain a more complete list of cases, searches were conducted of larger newspapers in the state. These searches substantially broadened the list of cases. Later, as more interviews were conducted with state police and county sheriffs, still more cases were identified. For cases discovered in this manner, newspaper articles were also obtained. Newspaper articles often provided more accurate and complete information than the personal recall of officials.

The product of this search was a list of seventy-four marijuana-growing cases in Illinois between 1980 and 1990 in which twenty or more plants were seized and in which at least one arrest was made. These seventy-four cases were drawn from forty-three of the state's 102 counties. This list is not exhaustive; it would be virtually impossible to find every case in Illinois from 1980 to 1990. The list does provide a representative range of cases during that period and probably includes most of the major cases in the state.

It was initially thought that records from the Illinois State Police (ISP) Cash Crop Program would be utilized to identify cases. However, some ISP officers were uncomfortable with this, and it was decided not to pursue this avenue and strain an otherwise good working relationship with the ISP. It turned out that such a listing would have been more complete but would have also left out some major cases, especially for the early 1980s. The Cash Crop Program, which collects such information, did not begin until 1983, and even after that some local law-enforcement agencies defined marijuana growing as a local problem and did not report cases to the ISP. The willingness of local police to cooperate with the ISP seems to have improved considerably by the late 1980s, when other sources of cases were also quite good. The decision not to pursue the ISP files also proved useful during interviews when subjects asked how we came to know about their case. Referring to newspaper clippings rather than police reports reinforced the fact that we were not part of any ongoing police investigation.

CASE OUTCOMES

After the list of seventy-four cases was obtained, another major task was to determine outcomes. Newspaper articles did not always follow a case to its conclusion. The process of determining case outcomes was slightly different for cases prosecuted at the state level and those prosecuted at the federal level. Of the seventy-four identified cases, fifty-three were handled at the state level, twenty were handled at the federal level, and one involved prosecuting the same offenders at both the state and federal levels.

To obtain the disposition on individual cases at the state level, circuit clerks were called. For two cases there were no records in the circuit clerk's office; an additional case was thrown out on a technicality; and two cases were still pending. This left forty-eight cases on the state level that were resolved and for which dispositions were available. On the federal level, obtaining the dispositions of the fourteen resolved cases was more difficult. If the disposition was not described in a newspaper account, it either required a personal visit to the federal court or the payment of a fee for court personnel to locate the docket sheet. Federal courts were visited in Benton, Peoria, and Rockford. At the conclusion of the study, seven cases at the federal level were still pending.

This case information was then coded and put into a database file. Items coded included county, year of arrest, age, sex, occupation of primary grower, number of plants grown, type of growing (whether indoor or outdoor), where plants were grown (on own land or elsewhere), and the disposition of the case (amount of fine, time given in jail, etc.). Except for occupation, fairly complete information was collected. Occupation was difficult to obtain, as this was not typically in court records or newspaper articles. Also, the marijuana plants confiscated were sometimes reported in number of pounds. To code these cases, the assumption was made that one plant equaled one pound.

LOCATING SUBJECTS

Given the nature of the interview questions, it did not seem proper, or in' the growers' best interest, to interview before the case was resolved and there was a formal recognition of guilt. After a case was resolved in court, the next step was to locate the grower and request an interview. This was not difficult in most cases, since many newspaper articles reported an address or an approximate location, and about 70 percent of the growers were listed in their local phone book. When growers were unlisted and it was not obvious where they lived, addresses were sometimes sought from public officials.

If the grower had a listed phone number, a letter was sent explaining the project and informing him or her that a staff member would call to provide more information and to arrange an interview. The letter stressed the research nature of the project and the federal grant of immunity that covered it. A few growers called, requesting more information. In most cases though, a staff member called a week or two later, giving the grower time to make a decision.

Growers with unlisted phone numbers were sent a letter explaining the project and asking them to call collect for more information. After about two weeks, growers who had not called were sent a a second letter, explaining the project in greater detail and asking them to reconsider and call collect. Of the nine contacts in this matter, one responded initially and one responded after the second letter. Since seven of the nine did not respond at all, it was concluded that contact by letter was not particularly successful.

Of the total letters sent, one was returned because the person had moved and there was no forwarding address, and in two cases we initially contacted an incorrect person. One of the latter cases was due to an incorrect name given verbally by a public official (an example of why we began to rely more on public written records) and the second was due to the unlikely occurrence of two people with the same name living on the same block.

Another possibility was that while the case was resolved, the grower was still in jail. Three of the subjects were in the state correctional system. To locate these inmates and obtain permission to interview them, we first contacted the Department of Public Affairs of the Illinois State Department of Corrections. Next, letters were sent to the inmates, explaining the project and asking them to call collect. All three contacted us and wished to be interviewed. We then sent a letter to the director of the Department of Corrections, explaining the study and requesting permission for the interviews.

As with finding case dispositions, trying to interview prisoners on the federal level proved more difficult, involving a fair amount of paperwork. To obtain permission to interview a federal prisoner, we sent a copy of the research proposal, interview schedule, and an implied consent form to the Federal Bureau of Prisons. They approved the request, the prisoner was then contacted, gave his consent, and the interview was conducted.

THE INTERVIEW

Interviews varied in length, but averaged one and a half hours. They were done by the primary researcher, generally at the convenience of the growers and at their homes. Each grower was paid $25 for the interview and given a federal grant of immunity, which guaranteed confidentiality and anonymity. Topics covered in the interview included circumstances of the arrest, how and why the person began growing, selling practices (if relevant), general views on marijuana, and the effects of the arrest on the person's life and relationships with their family, friends, and community. All but one of the growers consented to having the interview taped, and all taped interviews were transcribed.

Approximately 60 percent of those contacted consented to be interviewed. Of the people who refused, the most common reason was that the event was too traumatic and they wanted to forget about it. A few expressed suspicion of our motives and intent. There were also a few who themselves would have agreed to an interview, but they reported being pressured by wives or family members not to cooperate. While we always emphasized the academic nature of the study and the federal grant of immunity that came with it, given the current war on drugs, it was not unreasonable for these people to be suspicious.

The motivations of the people who consented were varied. Some felt they had been mistreated by the legal system and wanted to tell their side. Others felt they had made a mistake and wanted people to learn from it. Still others were curious and just thought the study sounded interesting. The payment of $25 was probably helpful in persuading people to consent to the interview, but it didn't appear to be a decisive factor. One person who refused said, "You could pay me $100, and I still wouldn't do this."

Transcribed interviews were then coded and stored on a database, so that summary information could be compiled. While much of the questionnaire was open-ended and could not be coded, there were many questions that could be put in coded form (for example, yes/no questions). Coding interviews proved to be more difficult than anticipated, as the questionnaire was long and changed several times over the course of the study. Consistency and comparability had to be maintained across time and interviews. This coded summary information was useful, although it was in the uncoded parts of the interview that the most interesting thoughts and ideas often occurred.

QUESTIONS OF ACCURACY

A major issue was whether the research procedures would yield an accurate picture of domestic marijuana growers. The issue of accuracy has several dimensions, including whether arrested growers are different from those who are undetected, whether arrested growers who cooperate are different from those who refuse to interview, and whether honest answers could be expected in a study of this type.

Arrested versus Undetected Growers

There is a question of whether arrested growers are markedly different from those not detected. It might be argued that a group of arrested growers would be weighted toward those who are inept at avoiding detection. While this sample may indeed have more than its share of naive growers, there are several justifications for using this group. First, this is an exploratory study intended to identify a *range* of grower types and to articulate general issues that may be further explored in subsequent studies. This research is not intended to reflect the *precise distribution* of these grower types or of grower characteristics. That is, the images are being painted in broad strokes rather than fine lines.

Second, many growers interviewed in this study had been involved for some time before their arrest—a median of five years with a few having grown for fifteen years or longer. As was seen in chapters 7 and 8, this group included growers with a broad range of technical sophistication about marijuana growing and the marijuana business. It would be a mistake to characterize this entire group as inept novices.

Third, growers were almost universal in their recognition that the greatest threats to their operations were from other people. Nearly all said that if they were to get back into the business they would tell almost no one, not even their closest friends. The importance of this was recognized by many of the arrested growers, but even the most careful were sometimes caught by simple "bad luck." For example, one indoor operation was discovered by firemen responding to a small fire in the house while the grower was away. Another grower had told only four other people but was turned in to the police by one of those people after a dispute between the two. Still others were discovered when their outdoor crops were stumbled upon by chance. For the most cautious even their closest friends who smoked marijuana with them often did not know they were growers. This obsession with secrecy by the most careful growers has important research implications regarding locating and interviewing growers who have not yet been arrested. Given their very small networks, it would be nearly impossible to identify them. Further, having identified them, they would be unwilling to talk, even with a grant of immunity. Consequently, even a sample of those not yet arrested is likely to be weighted toward those most willing to talk about what they do—that is, those most careless or uninitiated in crime.

The secrecy that surrounds commercial marijuana growing, combined with the fact that it largely occurs in rural settings, means that some of the techniques used to study urban drug use and urban drug networks would be less useful for studying this group. For example, in their study of daily marijuana users, Hendin et al. (1987) located subjects by using newspaper advertisements. Such an approach would not be practical in sparsely populated rural settings in which growers are not only secretive but widely dispersed.

Interviewed Growers versus Refusers

A second component of accuracy is whether interviewed growers are representative of *arrested* growers in general. Of the fifty-one resolved cases in this study in which a contact was made by letter and/or by telephone, it was possible to compare the refusers with interviewees on several characteristics, including age, sex, year of arrest, number of plants seized, type of operation (indoor versus outdoor), whether the plants were grown on their own land, the county in which the plants were grown, and the case disposition. Except for region and year of arrest, there were no systematic differences between those who refused and those who agreed to interviews. In the southern quarter refusals outnumbered consents by two-to-one, while in the remainder of the state, consents outnumbered refusals by two-to-one. This may be relevant since it is the southern part of the state that has a history of moonshining and a general disregard for formal law (Angle, 1980), and it is in the south where marijuana growing seems most frequent (see chapter 6).

There were also differences in the willingness of growers to cooperate according to the year in which they were arrested. In general, the older the case, the less likely they were to cooperate. When contacted by phone, these growers indicated they had finally put the arrest behind them and did not want to be reminded of it.

Honest Answers?

There is also a question of whether interviewed growers were truthful in their responses. From the start it was understood that growers and police officials viewed the issue of marijuana growing differently and their perspectives would color their responses. The emotional involvement of some growers and the commitment of officials were constant reminders that perspective would be an important consideration in interpreting answers.

Separate from the issue of perspective is that of outright deception. In some cases growers and officials presented different versions of events, but the objective "truth" was impossible for the researcher to determine. For example, four of the growers interviewed maintained their innocence throughout their interviews. One said it was a brother who was growing it, but there was parental pressure for him to take the blame, and the arrest was now an issue that divided the family. Another claimed his farm worker grew it and set him up. The two others stated they had rented the land out, and their tenants were growing it. These four saw the interview as a chance to set the record straight, and several maintained that the police knew (or should have known) they were innocent but needed a scapegoat. In contrast, interviewed officials expressed little doubt of their guilt. From the researcher's perspective, there is no way to judge with certainty what actually occurred. Interviews were conducted with these people and, apart from the "truth" of their guilt or innocence, these interviews proved useful in regard to the community response to the arrest.

Wary of distortions that might arise from the subjects' perspective, or from outright lying, several precautions were taken. First, interviews were not only conducted with growers but with police, newspaper reporters, and even a well-known author of how-to books on marijuana growing. In short, anyone with knowledge about marijuana growers was sought out for an interview. Second, no single statement by anyone (whether grower or police) was taken at face value. Instead, the constant search was for patterns or recurring themes. Statements that stood in contrast to general patterns were considered anomalies or special cases and were given secondary consideration in the absence of corroborative sources.

INTERVIEWS WITH OFFICIALS

In addition to interviews with arrested growers, law-enforcement officers familiar with marijuana grower cases were also interviewed. These included members of the Illinois State Police, county sheriffs, the National Forest Service, the DEA, two federal prosecutors, and a local prosecutor. Several interviews were also conducted with officials in Kentucky, Indiana, Missouri, Tennessee, and Hawaii to put the study in a broader context. These interviews focused mainly on general issues related to marijuana growing, although some questions were asked about specific cases. Examples of some of the issues raised during the interviews were: the extent of marijuana growing in the area; the kinds of people involved in growing; changing patterns in growing; the danger marijuana growers posed for law-enforcement officials and the community as a whole; the extent to which marijuana growing could be eradicated in the area, and so on. In general, these interviews were not as structured as the interviews with growers.

OTHER INTERVIEWS

In addition to growers and law-enforcement officials, the initial study had proposed short interviews with several citizens from each community in which a grower had been arrested. The intent was to supplement grower reports about community response, to determine how rural communities support or reject long-time members arrested for growing marijuana. This proved to be the most difficult task of the project and it was fortunate that the research did not hinge on successful interviews with community members. There were several problems in locating and interviewing community members. The most serious problem was the general unwillingness of citizens in rural communities to talk about the misfortune or misbehavior of fellow community members. In one community frustration with finding citizens to interview led to a decision to first interview a police officer who was well known and respected in the community. More than two months of repeated efforts failed to produce an interview with the officer. He was willing to be interviewed about police procedure and technical details of the case but was uncomfortable talking about the community response to the arrest and the way in which citizens changed their views of the offender following the arrest. A request to the officer's supervisor generated a similar response. In another community the local sheriff said a farmer had been arrested for growing marijuana in the county but that he (the sheriff) and the local prosecutor had discussed the matter and decided they would not discuss the case or even give the name of the farmer.

In still another instance a sheriff's deputy was asked about a case for which the researcher had only sketchy information. The deputy replied that his job would be in jeopardy if he discussed the case or even gave the names of the arrested growers, two established members of the community.

The reluctance of citizens to talk about the criminal activities of their rural neighbors is not unique to the study of marijuana growers. In his oral history of homicides in rural Kentucky, Montell (1986) describes the problems of getting citizens to talk about rural homicides, even as much as sixty years after the event. His work also illustrates the importance of informal networks for gaining entry to these groups.

A second problem with community interviews was that several growers, particularly those with no prior arrests, were concerned that community interviews would rekindle public animosity and compel them to relive the public embarrassment of their arrest. The researcher felt strongly that the project should neither protect nor punish growers (or police for that matter) who cooperated with the study. To cause further harm to individuals already convicted and punished by the law would raise ethical questions and might jeopardize future interviews. Considering the reluctance of citizens to cooperate and the potential harm to growers who had agreed to take part in the study, it was decided to give citizen interviews a low priority.

Though much of the focus was on interviewing growers and criminal justice officials, others familiar with the domestic marijuana industry were also interviewed. These individuals included authors of books on growing marijuana, the editors of two magazines on marijuana and marijuana growing, and three people who had served as director of the National Organization for the Reform of Marijuana Laws. These people provided yet another perspective on the problem and their input was used to confirm or deny patterns the researcher thought were emerging from the study. They also provided a national perspective on the issue.

Appendix B

FEDERAL MARIJUANA LAWS

PART 1: SUMMARY OF FEDERAL MARIJUANA LAWS—USC 1982, TITLE 21

Penalty for manufacture of marijuana, distribution of marijuana, or possession of marijuana, with intent to manufacture or distribute: (Sec 841)

    I. First offense:

        A. Up to 5 years imprisonment

        B. Up to $15,000 fine

        C. At least 2 years special parole, if given imprisonment

    II. Prior felony drug offense:

        A. Up to 10 years imprisonment

        B. Up to $30,000 fine

        C. At least 4 years special parole, if given imprisonment

If marijuana involved exceeds 1,000 pounds (454 kilograms), the penalty can be:

    I. First offense:

        A. Up to 15 years imprisonment

        B. Up to $125,000 fine

    II. Prior felony drug offense:

        A. Up to 30 years imprisonment

        B. Up to $250,000 fine

If a person distributes a small amount of marijuana for no remuneration, the offense is treated as a simple possession. The penalty for simple possession (Sec 844) is:

    I. First offense:

        A. No more than 1 year imprisonment

        B. No more than $5000 fine

II. Prior offense:
    A. No more than 2 years imprisonment
    B. No more than $10,000 fine
For a first time offender, a person may be put on probation, and if he does not violate probation, then the court may dismiss proceedings against him. The Department of Justice keeps a non-public record of the offense, solely for purposes of determining prior offense, in case of subsequent proceedings.

Distribution to Persons under 21: (Sec 845)

Can be punishable up to twice term of imprisonment, fine or parole, if first time offender. Can be punishable up to three times term of imprisonment, fine or parole, if prior offender.

Attempt and Conspiracy: (Sec 846)

Any person who attempts or conspires to commit any of the prior offenses can be punished as if he committed the offense.

Continuing Criminal Enterprise: (Sec 848)

A person can be charged with CCE if he commits a felony offense, and such violation is a part of a continuing series of violations, of which he acted in concert with five or more other people, had a management type position in the enterprise, and obtained substantial income from the enterprise. Punishment for CCE is imprisonment from ten years to life, and fines up to $100,000. If person has prior CCE offense, imprisonment is from twenty years to life, with fines up to $200,000.

Forfeiture: (Sec 881)

The following items can be subject to forfeiture: (1) all controlled substances (2) raw materials, products and equipment, used to manufacture or deliver the substances (3) property used as a container for the substances (4) all conveyances (aircraft, ships, vehicles) used to transport the substances (5) all books, records, and research and (6) money, securities, or other things of value which were exchanged for controlled substances.

PART 2: SUMMARY OF FEDERAL MARIJUANA LAWS—USC 1988, TITLE 21

Penalties for manufacture of marijuana, distribution of marijuana, or possession of marijuana with intent to manufacture or distribute: (Sec 841)

I.   Less than 50 kilograms of a mixture or substance containing a detectable amount of marijuana or less than 50 plants
- A. First offense:
  1. Up to 5 years imprisonment
  2. Up to $250,000 fine
  3. At least 2 year special parole, if given imprisonment
- B. Prior felony drug offense:
  1. Up to 10 years imprisonment
  2. Up to $500,000 fine
  3. At least 4 years supervised release, if given imprisonment

II. 50 or more kilograms and less than a 100 kilograms of a mixture or substance containing a detectable amount of marijuana or 50–99 plants
- A. First offense:
  1. Up to 20 years imprisonment
  2. Up to $1,000,000 fine
  3. At least 3 years supervised release, if given imprisonment
- B. Prior felony drug offense:
  1. Up to 30 years imprisonment
  2. Up to $2,000,000 fine
  3. At least 6 years supervised release, if given imprisonment

III. 100 kilograms or more and less than 100 kilograms of a mixture or substance containing a detectable amount of marijuana, or 100–999 plants.
- A. First offense:
  1. Between 5 years and 40 years imprisonment
  2. Up to $2,000,000 fine
  3. At least 4 years supervised release
- B. Prior felony drug offense:
  1. Between 10 years and life imprisonment
  2. Up to $4,000,000 fine
  3. At least 8 years supervised release

The sentence can not be suspended. Nor can the person be eligible for parole during imprisonment.

IV. 1000 kilograms or more of a mixture or substance containing a detectable amount of marijuana or 1000 or more plants

A. First offense:
    1. Between 10 years and life imprisonment
    2. Up to $4,000,000 fine
    3. At least 5 years supervised release
B. Second felony drug offense:
    1. Between 20 years and life imprisonment
    2. Up to $8,000,000 fine
    3. At least 10 years supervised release
C. More than two felony drug offenses:
    1. Mandatory life imprisonment

The sentence can not be suspended. Nor can a person be eligible for parole during his imprisonment.

V.   Distribution of a small amount of marijuana without remuneration is treated as a simple possession.

VI.   Any person who cultivates a controlled substance on Federal Property shall be imprisoned and fined as provided in this section. Any person who places a booby trap on Federal property in association with cultivation can be sentenced up to 10 years prison and fined up to $10,000 for a first time offender, to 20 years prison and up to $20,000 for a prior offender.

The penalties for simple possession (Sec 844 & 844a) are:

A. First offense:
    1. Up to 1 year sentence
    2. A minimum of a $1000 fine
B. Second drug offense:
    1. Between 15 days and 2 years sentence
    2. A minimum of a $2500 fine
C. Three or more drug offenses:
    1. Between 90 days and 3 years sentence
    2. A minimum of a $5000 fine

A civil penalty, not to exceed $10,000, can be assessed instead for possession of small amounts. A civil penalty may not be assessed if the person has a prior drug conviction. This civil penalty can be expunged from the record on a first offense after three years, if the individual pays the assessment, does not have any other drug offenses, and a drug test shows the individual to be drug fee. A nonpublic record of the disposition is then kept solely for purposes of determining prior offense, in case of subsequent offenses.

Distribution to Persons under 21: (Sec 845)

Can be punishable up to twice term of imprisonment, fine, or parole, if first time offender. For prior offenders, punishment can be up to three times term of imprisonment, fine, or parole. A minimum of one year sentence is required for either prior or first time offenders, unless offense involves 5 grams of marijuana or less.

Distribution or manufacture within 1000 feet of a public or private school or within 100 feet of a playground, youth center, public swimming pool, or video arcade: (Sec 845a)

Punishment is same as distribution to persons under 21, except that for prior offender, a minimum of 3 year sentence is required.

Attempt and Conspiracy: (Sec 846)

Any person who attempts or conspires to commit any of the above offenses is subject to the penalties prescribed for the offense

Continuing Criminal Enterprise: (Sec 848)

Any person who engages in continuing criminal enterprise shall be sentenced to a term ranging from 20 years to life imprisonment, and can be fined up to $2,000,000. If he has a prior conviction for CCE, sentence shall be 30 years to life, and fines can be up to $4,000,000. Sentence can not be suspended and probation is prohibited. Continuing Criminal Enterprise is defined as in USC Code 1982.

Death Penalty: (Sec 848e)

Any person who engages in CCE or in large scale distribution or production (1000 kg or greater) and intentionally kills or causes the killing of an individual, or any person who intentionally kills or causes the killing of a law enforcement official while engaging in any felony drug offense, shall be sentenced to prison for not less than 20 years, and up to life imprisonment, or can be sentenced to death.

Forfeiture: (Sec 853 & Sec 881)

Criminal forfeiture is mentioned, where it is stated that any person convicted of a drug violation punishable by imprisonment for more than one year shall forfeit to the United States any property, derived from any proceeds the person obtained as the result of such violation, or that was used (or intended to be used) to commit the violation. Under civil forfeiture, besides the items listed in USC 1982, a provision was also added to include all real property, which was used (or intended to be used) to commit a drug violation.

Denial of Government Benefits: (Sec 853a)

Any individual who is convicted of a Federal or State offense consisting of the distribution of controlled substances can upon the first conviction be ineligible for any or all Federal benefits for up to 5 years after conviction; for a second conviction, be ineligible for up to 10 years, and for a third or subsequent conviction, be permanently ineligible for all Federal benefits. For possession, upon the first conviction, a person may be ineligible for any or all Federal benefits for up to one year, for prior convictions up to 5 years. Federal benefits mean the issuance of any grant, contract, loan, professional or commercial license, and does not include retirement, welfare, Social Security, health, disability, veterans benefits, public housing, or other similar benefits.

BIBLIOGRAPHY

Abel, E. L. (1976). *A comprehensive guide to the cannabis literature*. Westport, CT: Greenwood Press.

———. (1980). *Marihuana: The first twelve thousand years*. New York: Plenum Press.

———. (1982). *A marihuana dictionary: Words, terms, events, and persons related to cannibis*. Westport, CT: Greenwood Press.

Adler, P. A. (1985). *Wheeling and dealing: An ethnography of an upper level drug dealing and smuggling community*. New York: Columbia University Press.

Anderson, H. (1985, Mar. 18). Drug wars: Murder in Mexico. *Newsweek*, 28–32.

Andrews, G., & Vinkenoog, S. (Eds.). (1967). *The book of grass: An anthology of Indian hemp*. New York: Grove Press.

Angle, P. M. (1980). *Bloody Williamson*. New York: Alfred A. Knopf.

Applebome, P. (1985, Sept.). What was farmer Brown doing with all that pot? *Texas Monthly*, 13:10, 11.

Bagley, B. M. (1988). Colombia and the war on drugs. *Foreign Affairs*, 67(1):70–92.

Becker, H. S. (1963). *Outsiders: Studies in the sociology of deviance*. New York: Free Press.

Bishop, K. (1990, Aug. 10). Military takes part in drug sweep and reaps criticism and a lawsuit. *New York Times*, A11.

Bonnie, R. J., & Whitebread, C. H., II. (1974). *The marihuana conviction: A history of marihuana prohibition in the United States*. Charlottesville: University Press of Virginia.

Boyle, T. C. (1984). *Budding prospects*. New York: Viking Press.

Brecher, E. M. (1972). Marijuana and hashish. in E.M. Brecher (Ed). *Licit and Illicit Drugs*. (395–472). Boston: Little, Brown and Company.

——. Drug laws and drug law enforcement: A review and evaluation based on 111 years of experience. *Drugs and Society*, 1(1):1–27.

Brown, E. J., Flanagan, T. J., & McLeod, M. (Eds.). (1984). *Sourcebook of criminal justice statistics—1983*. U.S. Department of Justice, Bureau of Justice Statistics. Washington, DC: U.S. Government Printing Office.

Castellano, T. C., & Uchida, C. D. (1990). Local drug enforcement, prosecutors and case attrition: Theoretical perspectives for the drug war. *American Journal of Police*, 9(1):133–62.

CBS News. (1989, Oct.). Home grown high. *48 Hours*.

Chapple, S. (1984). *Outlaws in Babylon: Shocking true adventures on America's marijuana frontier*. London, UK: Angus & Robertson.

Chopra, G. S. (1969). Man and marijuana. *The International Journal of the Addictions*, 4(2):215–247.

Clarke, R. C. (1981). *Marijuana botany*. Berkeley, CA: And/Or Press.

Climates of the states. (2nd ed.). (1980). Detroit, MI: Gale Research Company.

DeFleur, L. B. (1975). Biasing influences on drug arrest records: Implications for deviance research. *American Sociological Review*, 40(1):88–103.

Drug Enforcement Administration (DEA). (1988). *1988 Domestic Cannabis Eradication/Suppression Program*.

——. (1990). *1990 Domestic Cannabis Eradication/Suppression Program*.

Egan, T. (1991, Feb. 5). Life, liberty, and maybe marijuana: Choosing sides in Alaska. *New York Times*, B1.

Epstein, E. J. (1973). *News from nowhere: Television and the news*. New York: Vintage Books.

Erickson, P. G. (1980). *Cannabis criminals: The social effects of punishment on drug users*. Toronto, Canada: Addiction Research Foundation.

——. (1989). Living with prohibition: Regular cannabis users, legal sanctions, and informal controls. *The International Journal of the Addictions*, 24(3):175–188.

Erickson, P. G., & Murray, G. F. (1989). The undeterred cocaine user: Intention to quit and its relationship to perceived legal and health threats. *Contemporary Drug Problems*, 16(2):141–156.

Fairburn, J. W., Liebman, J. A., & Rowan, M. G. (1976). The stability of cannabis and its preparations on storage. *Journal of Pharmaceutical Pharmacology*, 28(1):1–7.

Falco, M. (1983, Dec. 11). The big business of illicit drugs. *New York Times Magazine*, 108–112.

Federal Bureau of Investigation (FBI). (1977). *Uniform crime reports*. Washington, DC: U.S. Government Printing Office.

——. (1989). *Uniform crime reports*. Washington, DC: U.S. Government Printing Office.

Fields, A. B. (1986). Weedslingers: Young black marijuana dealers. In G. Beschner & A. S. Friedman (Eds.). *Teen drug use*. (85–104). Lexington, MA: D. C. Heath.

First death sentence under new drug law. (1991, May 15). *New York Times*, A11.

Forest Service. (1988). *National forest system drug control program: 1988*. Washington, DC: U.S. Department of Agriculture.

———. (1989). *National forest system drug control program: 1989*. Washington, D. C.: U. S. Department of Agriculture.

Frank, M. (1988). *Marijuana grower's insider's guide*. Los Angeles, CA: Red Eye Press.

———. (1989, Jan.). Selecting a variety to grow. *High Times*, 43–49, 68.

Frank, M., & Rosenthal, E. (1978). *Marijuana grower's guide*. (Deluxe edition). Berkeley, CA: And/Or Press.

Frazier, J. (1974). *The marijuana farmers: Hemp cults and cultures*. New Orleans, LA: Solar Age Press.

Furnas, L. D., & Bartle, D. E. (1988). Homegrown destruction—Indiana's marijuana eradication program. *The Police Chief*, 55(6):24, 26–29.

Galliher, J. F., & Cross, J. R. (1982). Symbolic severity in the land of easy virtue: Nevada's high marihuana penalty. *Social Problems*, 29(4):380–386.

Galliher, J. F., & Walker, A. (1977). The puzzle of the social origins of the Marihuana Tax Act of 1937. *Social Problems*, 24(3):367–76.

Gallup, G., Jr. (1985, June 20). *The Gallup poll*. Princeton, NJ: Gallup.

Gettman, J. B. (1987). *Marijuana in America—1986*. Washington, DC: National Organization for the Reform of Marijuana Laws. (NORML).

Goldman, A. (1979). *Grass roots: Marijuana in America today*. New York: Harper & Row.

Gooberman, L. A. (1974). *Operation Intercept: The multiple consequences of public policy*. New York: Pergamon Press.

Goode, E. (1970). *The marijuana smokers*. New York: Basic Books.

Grinspoon, L. (1977). *Marijuana reconsidered*. (2nd ed.). Cambridge, MA: Harvard University Press.

Hendin, H., Haas, A. P., Singer, P., Ellner, M., & Ulman, R. (1987). *Living high: Daily marijuana use among adults*. New York, NY: Human Sciences Press.

Herer, J. (1990). *Hemp and the marijuana conspiracy: The emperor wears no clothes*. Van Nuys, CA: HEMP Publishing.

Himmelstein, J. L. (1983). *The strange career of marihuana: Politics and ideology of drug control in America*. Westport, CT: Greenwood Press.

———. (1986). The continuing career of marijuana: backlash . . . within limits. *Contemporary Drug Problems*, 13(1):1–21.

Illinois Revised Statutes, 1989, Vol. 2, Chaps. 38 & 56 1/2, State Bar Association Edition.

Inaba, D. (1987). Marijuana '87—A new drug. *Recovering*, 1(1):16.

Inciardi, J. (1981). Marijuana decriminalization research. *Criminology*, 19(1):145-59.

———. (1986). *The war on drugs: Heroin, cocaine, crime, and public policy*. Palo Alto, CA: Mayfield.

Inciardi, J. A., & McBride, D. C. (1989). Legalization: A high risk alternative in the war on drugs. *American Behavioral Scientist*, 32(3):259-289.

Jehl, D. (1990, May 16). Back yard brawl in drug war. *Los Angeles Times*, A1, A14.

Johnson, F. (1989, Dec. 17). High in the hollows. *New York Times Magazine*. 30, 46, 47, 49, 51.

Johnson, S. (1989, Oct. 24). Vermont ponders spirit of the law on drugs. *New York Times*, 8.

Johnston, L. D., O'Malley, P. M., & Bachman, J. G. (1986). *Drug use among American high school students, college students, and other young adults: Natonal trends through 1985*. U.S. Department of Health and Human Services, National Institute on Drug Abuse. Washington, DC: U.S. Government Printing Office.

———. (1988). *Illicit drug use, smoking, and drinking by America's high school students, college students, and young adults, 1975-1987*. U.S. Department of Health and Human Services, National Institute on Drug Abuse. Washington, DC: U.S. Government Printing Office.

Kelly, J. (1989, July 11). 40% in the county said to grow weed. *USA Today*, 1A-2A.

———. (1990, July 20). Grass-roots campaigns: Candidates want pot legalized. *USA Today*, 2A.

Kessler, M. (1990). Expanding legal services programs to rural America: A case study of program creation and operations. *Judicature*, 73(5):273-80.

Kleiman, M. A. (1989). *Marijuana: Costs of abuse, costs of control*. Westport, CT: Greenwood Press.

Knox farmer pleads guilty to marijuana-growing charge. (1987, Aug. 28). *Peoria Journal-Star*, A5.

Koski, P. R., & Eckberg, D. L. (1983). Bureaucratic legitimation: Marihuana and the Drug Enforcement Administration. *Sociological Focus*, 16(4):255-73.

Langer, J. (1977). Drug entrepreneurs and dealing culture. *Social Problems*, 24(3):377-86.

Lawn, J. C. (1984). *Cultivation and eradication of illicit domestic marijuana*. U.S. Congressional Report. Washington, DC: U.S. Government Printing Office.

———. (1985). The DEA's role in the prevention of drug trafficking and abuse. *Police Chief*, 52(10):31-32, 34, 36, 39, 40-41.

Lawren, B. (1985). Killer weed. *Omni*, 7(12):16, 106.

Littlewood, T. B. (1969). *Horner of Illinois*. Evanston, IL: Northwestern University Press.

Mandel, J. (1988). Is marijuana law enforcement racist? *Journal of Psychoactive Drugs*, 20(1):83–91.

Mann, P. (1985). *Marijuana alert*. New York: McGraw-Hill.

Manning, P. K., & Redlinger, L. J. (1983). Drugs as work. In I. Harper Simpson & R. L. Simpson (Eds.). *Research in the sociology of work*. (275–300). Greenwich, CT: JAI Press.

Marsasak, L. (1988, Sept. 23). House OK's harsh penalties for recreational drug users. *Decatur Herald & Review*. A1.

Matza, D. (1964). *Delinquency and drift*. New York: John Wiley & Sons.

McHugh, P. (1986, July 28). Retaking the marijuana trail. *San Francisco Chronicle*, 63, 65.

Merlin, M. D. (1972). *Man and marijuana: Some aspects of their ancient relationship*. Rutherford, NJ: Fairleigh Dickinson University Press.

Mieczkowski, T. (1986). Geeking up and throwing down: Heroin street life in Detroit. *Criminology*, 24(4):645–66.

Mikuriya, T. H., & Aldrich, M. R. (1988). Cannabis 1988: Old drug, new dangers, the potency question. *Journal of Psychoactive Drugs*, 20(1):47–55.

Mills, J. (1986). *The underground empire: Where crime and governments embrace*. New York: Dell.

Montell, W. L. (1986). *Killings: Folk justice in the upper South*. Lexington, KY: University of Kentucky Press.

Mouledoux, J. (1972). Ideological aspects of a drug dealership. In K. Westhues (Ed.). *Society's shadow: Studies in the sociology of counter cultures*. New York: McGraw-Hill.

Musto, D. (1973). *The American disease: Origins of narcotic control*. New Haven: Yale University Press.

National Narcotics Intelligence Consumers Committee (NNICC). (1984). *The NNICC report 1984: The supply of illicit drugs to the United States from foreign and domestic sources in 1984*.

――――. (1985–86). *The NNICC report 1985–86: The supply of illicit drugs to the United States from foreign and domestic sources in 1985 and 1986*.

――――. (1987). *The NNICC report 1987: The supply of illicit drugs to the United States from foreign and domestic sources in 1987*.

――――. (1988). *The NNICC report 1988: The supply of illicit drugs to the United States from foreign and domestic sources in 1988*.

――――. (1989). *The NNICC report 1989: The supply of illicit drugs to the United States from foreign and domestic sources in 1989*.

――――. (1990). *The NNICC report 1990: The supply of illicit drugs to the United States from foreign and domestic sources in 1990*.

Office of National Drug Control Policy. (1989). *National drug control strategy*. Washington, DC: U. S. Government Printing Office.

Passell, P. (1989, Sept. 5). The high hidden costs of the war on marijuana. *The New York Times*, A14.

Potter, G., & Gaines, L. (1990). *Organizing crime in "Copperhead County": An ethnographic look at rural crime networks*. Paper presented at the meeting of the Southern Sociological Association, Louisville, KY.

Potter, G., Gaines, L., & Holbrook, B. (1989). *Blowing smoke: An evaluation of marijuana enforcement in Kentucky*. Paper presented at the meeting of the International Conference on Drug Policy Reform, Washington, DC.

Preble, E., & Casey, J. J., Jr. (1969). Taking care of business—The heroin user's life on the street. *The International Journal of the Addictions*, 4(1):1–24.

Raphael, R. (1985). *Cash crop: An American dream*. Mendocino, CA: Ridge Times Press.

Reininger, W. (1966). Historical notes. In D. Solomon (Ed.). *The Marihuana Papers* (100–101). Indianapolis: Bobbs–Merrill Co.

Reuter, P., MacCoun, R., & Murphy, P. (1990). *Money from crime: A study of the economics of drug dealing in Washington, D.C.* Santa Monica, CA: RAND Corporation.

Rise in marijuana cultivation on federal land is reported. (1984, Dec. 13). *New York Times*, 10.

Robins, L. N., Helzer, J. E., & Davis, D. H. (1975). Narcotic use in Southeast Asia and afterward. *Archives of General Psychiatry*, 32(8):955–61.

Rosevar, J. (1967). *Pot: A handbook of marijuana*. New York: University Books.

Schultes, R. E., Klein, W. M., Plowman, T., & Lockwood, T. E. (1974). *Cannabis: An example of taxonomic neglect*. Botanical Museum Leaflets, Harvard University. 23(9):337–64. cited in M. Frank & E. Rosenthal (1978). *Marijuana grower's guide*. (Deluxe edition). Berkeley, CA: And/Or Press.

Selgnij, S., & Clarke, R. C. (1988). Ruderalis—Friend or foe? *The Best of High Times, Volume VI*. 14.

Shabecoff, P. (1986, Oct. 31). Plan unveiled to curb boom in marijuana from U.S. land. *New York Times*, 1, 12.

Sinoway, R. (1987). Seizure of houses and real property under marijuana forfeiture laws. *Search and Seizure Law Report*, 14(4):113–20.

Six Kentucky law officers arrested on drug charges. (1990, Aug. 29). *Narcotics Control Digest*, 4-5.

Slaughter, J. B. (1988). Marijuana prohibition in the United States: History and analysis of a failed policy. *Columbia Journal of Law and Social Problems*, 51(4):417-74.

Smith, W. (1987, Sept. 10). Marijuana seized down on farm. *Chicago Tribune*, 3.

Solomon, D. (1966).   The marihuana myths. in D. Solomon (Ed). *The Marihuana Papers*. (xiii–xxi) Indianapolis: Bobbs–Merrill Co.

Stamler, R. T., Fahlman, R. C., & Vigeant, H. (1985).   Illicit traffic and abuse of cannabis in Canada. *Bulletin on Narcotics*, 37(4):37–49.

Taylor, N. (1966).   The pleasant assassin: The story of marihuana.   In D. Solomon (Ed.).   *The marihuana papers*. (3-17).   Indianapolis, IN: The Bobbs–Merrill Co.

Trebach, A. (1987).   *The great drug war*. New York: Macmillan.

United States Code, Title 21, 1982.

United States Code, Title 21, 1988.

United States Department of Agriculture. (1944).   *Agricultural statistics: 1944*. Washington, DC: U.S. Government Printing Office.

———. (1945).   *Agricultural statistics: 1945*. Washington, DC: U.S. Government Printing Office.

———. (1946).   *Agricultural statistics: 1946*. Washington, DC: U.S. Government Printing Office.

———. (1990).   *Crop values: 1989 summary*. Washington, DC: U.S. Government Printing Office.

U.S. says Mexico's production of marijuana was underestimated. (1990, Feb. 27).   *New York Times*, A7.

Violent gardeners. (1986).   *U.S. News & World Report*, 101(14):63.

Wallach, L. (1989).   The chemistry of reefer madness. *Omni*, 11(11):18, 64.

Walton, R. P. (1938). *Marihuana: America's new drug problem*.   Philadelphia: Lippincot.   Reprinted in 1976, New York: Arno Press.

Warner, R. (1986). *Invisible hand: The marijuana business*.   New York: Beech Tree Books.

Weinberg, D. (1987).   Rural pockets of poverty. *Rural Sociology*, 52:399–408.

Weisheit, R. A. (1990).   Domestic marijuana: Mainstreaming deviance. *Deviant Behavior*.   11:107–29.

———. (1991a).   The intangible rewards from crime: The case of domestic marijuana cultivation. *Crime and Delinquency*.   37(4):506–527.

———. (1991b).   Drug use among marijuana growers. *Contemporary Drug Problems*.   18(2):191–217.

———. (in press).   Drugs and crime: What if . . . .   In J. M. Klofas and S. Stojkovic (Eds.). *Crime and Justice in the Year 2010*.   Pacific Grove, CA: Brooks/Cole Publishing Co.

Weisheit, R. A., & Johnson, K. (in press). Exploring the dimensions of support for decriminalizing drugs. *Journal of Drug Issues*.

Williams, S. (1987, Aug. 19).   Raid uncovers giant marijuana farm. *Peoria Journal-Star*, A1, A2.

Williams, T. (1989). *The cocaine kids*. New York: Addison-Wesley.

Wisconsin teens using more LSD. (1987, May 14). *Chicago Tribune*, 3.

Wolkomir, R., & Wolkomir, J. (1988, Oct.).   Drug outlaws in our national
    forests. *Reader's Digest*, 193–94, 197–98, 200.
Zinberg, N. (1984).   *Drug, set, and setting: The basis for controlled intoxicant
    use*. New Haven, CT: Yale University Press.

INDEX

Addicts and addiction, 17, 40, 88, 91, 114, 120, 127
Adler, Patricia, 91
Afghanistan, 71
Africa, 12–14, 19
Alcohol, 8, 12–14, 16, 18, 21, 46, 112–18, 127, 132, 152
Alabama, 22, 38
Alaska, 24
Aldrich, Michael, 56–57
Amotivational syndrome, 25
Amphetamines, 117, 132
Angel, Paul, 63
Anslinger, Harry, 21
Anti-Drug Abuse Act, 26
Anti-Drug Abuse Amendment Act, 26
Arab, 12–13
Arizona, 2
Armstrong, Louis, 18
Asia, 11, 13, 19, 50
Autotitration, 56

Bagley, Bruce, 84
Bahamas, 9
Becker, Howard, 18
Bible, 13
Black market, 46

Booby traps, 26, 38, 47, 50, 107, 132, 142–43, 150, 156; *Also see* Violence
Boyle, T. Coraghessan, 40, 42
Brazil, 14
Buckley, William F., Jr., 22, 24
Budding Prospects, 42
Bush, George, 16

California, 9, 25, 38, 40, 44, 50, 62, 64, 70, 72, 129, 132, 138
Campaign Against Marijuana Planting, 139
CAMP. *See* Campaign Aginst Marijuana Planting
Canada, 1
Cannabis indica, 53–55, 57, 94; *See also* Marijuana
Cannabis ruderalis, 54, 58; *See also* Marijuana
Cannabis sativa, 53–55, 57, 94; *See also* Marijuana
Carter, President Jimmy, 22
Casey, John, 88
Cash Crop Program, 64–65
Cash crops: Marijuana as a, 34–35, 51; Legitimate crops, 34–35, 40

Castellano, Thomas, 3
Chapple, Steve, 50
China, 11–12, 19
Citizens Observation Group, 129
Civil War and hemp, 15–16
Coca, 7, 38
Cocaine, 2–6, 19, 21, 25, 50–51,
    84, 91, 108, 117, 119–21, 127,
    136, 143–45, 157–58
Codeine, 6
COG. *See* Citizens Observation
    Group
Colombia, 7, 49, 144
Commercial growers, 10
Communal growers, 45–47, 76, 88,
    99; *See also* typology of growers
Comprehensive Crime Control Act,
    26
Comprehensive Drug Abuse Pre-
    vention and Control Act, 22
Conservatives 23–24
Conspicuous consumption, 5–6
Continuing Criminal Enterprise
    Law, 26
Corruption of officials, 49, 151–53,
    157
Crack. *See* Cocaine

Daniel Boon National Forest, 38
Declaration of Independence, 11
Decriminalization 6, 19, 22–25,
    112–16, 120, 129–30, 145, 152,
    155
DEA. *See* Drug Enforcement Ad-
    ministration
Decoy plots, 150–51
Department of Agriculture, 15
Ditchweed. *See* hemp, wild mari-
    juana
Domestic Cannabis Produc-
    tion/Suppression Program. *See*
    Domestic Marijuana Eradication
    Program

Domestic Marijuana Eradication
    Program, 1, 35, 39, 54
Domestic marijuana industry, 1–3,
    5
Drug dealing 3–5, 7, 40–41, 53, 73,
    88, 91, 118, 120, 132, 158
Drug Enforcement Administration,
    1–2, 22–23, 25, 31, 39–40, 49,
    54, 57, 59, 63, 65, 135, 138, 148,
    150
Drug policies, 7
Drug testing, 25, 27
Drug treatment, 120

The Emperor Wears No Clothes, 89
England, 15, 19
Eradication of marijuana, 1, 3, 25,
    39, 49, 63–64, 70, 136, 147, 153;
Erickson, Patricia, 109, 116, 119
Europe, 12–14, 19

Farmers, 5, 8–9, 15, 27, 40, 42–43,
    73, 79, 83, 99, 102, 113, 115,
    124–25, 128
Farmers Home Administration, 29
Federal Bureau of Investigation, 6
Federal Bureau of Narcotics, 17
Federal land, marijuana growing
    on. *See* National forests
Firearms. *See* Guns
Florida, 25
Forfeiture, 10, 26–29, 138, 147,
    153, 155; Civil 27;
Frazier, Jack, 13

Georgia, 22
Ginzburg, Douglas, 7
Greeks, 13
Greenhouses, 59; *See also* Marijua-
    na, indoor growing
Guns and weapons, 47, 50, 91,
    109–112, 142, 150, 156, 158
Gutenberg Bible, 11

Hashish, 13, 15, 49, 117, 132
Hashishin, 13
Hawaii, 7–8, 25, 38, 135, 148–50, 152
Hemp, 2, 10–12, 14–15, 19, 47, 53–56, 58, 68, 78, 89, 97, 149; Chinese and, 12; Hemp cults, 13
Herer, Jack, 16
Heroin, 3, 5–6, 8, 21, 117, 119–20, 136, 144–45, 158
High Times, 41, 81–82
Holland, 81
Horticulture and marijuana growing, 43, 80, 82, 92, 99
Hustlers, 41–43, 46, 75–76; *See also* Typology of growers
Hydroponics, 60, 80, 90

Illinois, 8, 10, 15, 30, 36, 38, 42, 59, 61–70, 72, 73, 76, 99, 100, 120, 130, 135, 137, 139, 142–43, 148, 150–152, 156
Illinois State Police, 64–65, 76, 104, 139; *See also* State police
India, 12
Indiana, 8, 15, 63, 135, 148–52
Indian Hemp Commission, 12
Indica. *See Cannabis Indica*
Indoor growing, 9, 59–60, 64, 74, 80, 82, 87, 99, 105, 143, 156;
Internal Revenue Service, 74
Intrinsic rewards from growing. *See* Rewards of growing
Iowa, 15
Irrigation, 9
ISP. *See* Illinois State Police

Jamaica, 49
Japanese, 15, 54

Kentucky, 3, 7–9, 15, 25, 38, 40, 45, 63–64, 70, 130, 132, 135, 148–52, 156–57; Hemp production, 15; Types of growers in, 45
King Range National Conservation Area, 138
Kleiman, Mark, 32, 36, 50

Langer, John, 91
Laws regarding marijuana, 26, 28; Cannabis trafficking, 28; Civil penalties, 27; Conspiracy, 26–28; Continuing Criminal Enterprise, 26; Denial of federal benefits, 26–27; Fines, 28–30, 126; Manufacture, 26, 28–29; Penalties 21–24, 26, 28; Possession, 22, 26–28; Probation, 30, 124–25; Sales 22, 26–27; Support for, 64
Legalization. *See* Decriminalization
Libertarians, 24
Linnaeus, Carl 53
Little Egypt, 63
Littlewood, Thomas, 63
Los Angeles Police Department, 17
LSD, 48, 117, 132, 145

Mandel, Jerry, 72
Marijuana: Books about, 24; Botany of, 10, 53–58, 80; Origins, 11–13; Use by children, 24, 46, 77–78, 98, 110, 114–16, 132, 145, 153; Commercial grade, 32, 34, 57, 59–60, 77; Cultivation, 2, 4, 26, 32; As a gateway drug, 24–25, 120; High school seniors, 18–19, 24, 78; Industrial uses of, 12, 15; Medical uses of, 6, 12–13, 15–17, 19; Military uses, 15; Morality of use, 112–14; Religious uses 12–13, 19; Sales to minors, 22, 26; Trends in use, 18–19; *See also* Eradication of marijuana; Potency of marijuana; Violence

Marijuana growers, drug use by, 101; reputation of, 121–26; self-esteem of, 128; social characteristics of, 71–74

Marijuana Grower's Guide, 82

Marijuana growing: Attrition, 58–59, 74; Avoiding detection,101–104; Books about, 28, 79–80, 82, 99; Climate and, 5, 55–56, 59–62, 70, 157; Cloning, 60, 80–82, 94–95; Commercial, 1, 5–6, 39, 41, 59, 69, 155; Economic incentives, 68–70, 76, 149, 155; Income from, 40, 45, 57, 74–75, 84, 99, 140; Morality of, 43, 112–14, 120; Penalties, 26; Regional variations, 10; Risk and, 42, 139, 141, 153; Technical knowledge of, 60, 74, 80–81; *See also* Indoor growing; Marijuana thieves; Pride in growing; Violence

Marijuana Tax Act, 15–16, 19, 21

Marijuana thieves, 47, 58, 59, 74, 84–87, 99, 103–5, 107–8, 110, 112, 132, 150

Matza, David, 114

Mexico as a producer nation, 2, 14, 19, 32, 38, 47–50

Mexican immigrants, 17, 21; *See also* Race

Mexican marijuana, 55

Michigan, 2

Middle East, 12–13, 19

Mikuriya, Todd, 56–57

Minnesota, 2, 15

Minorities. *See* Race

Miranda rights, 147

Missouri, 8, 25, 38, 63, 135, 148–52

Moonshine, 62, 118, 150

Morphine, 6

Murder. *See* Marijuana violence

Murray, Glenn, 119

Mushrooms, 117

National Commission on Marijuana and Drug Abuse, 22

National Drug Control Strategy, 3

National Federation of Parents for Drug Free Youth, 24

National forests, 29, 38–39, 135, 148

National Geographic, 106

National Institute on Drug Abuse, 22

National Narcotics Intelligence Consumers Committee, 1, 32, 35, 49

National Organization for the Reform of Marijuana Laws, 8, 24, 39, 128

Nebraska, 22, 38

Netherlands, 77

Nevada, 22

New marijuana. *See* Potency of marijuana

New Mexico, 2

New Orleans, 18

New right, 23

New York, 72, 121

NNICC. *See* National Narcotics Intelligence Consumers Committee

NORML. *See* National Organization for the Reform of Marijuana Laws

North Africa, 49

Office of National Drug Control Policy, 3

Oklahoma, 38, 40

Operation Intercept, 47–50

Oregon, 24–25

Organic gardening, 43, 80, 82

Organic Gardening, 81

Organized crime, 46, 155

Paraphernalia, 24, 82
Paraquat, 47, 49–50
PCP, 117
Penalties for marijuana. *See* Laws;
Philipines and hemp, 15, 54
Photoperiod, 58–59
Pilgrims and hemp, 15
Potency of marijuana, 2, 16, 32–34,
    53–57, 59–60, 78, 91, 95–96, 98,
    156;
Poverty, 3
Pragmatists, 43–45, 76–77, 95; *See
    also* Typology of growers
Preble, Edward, 88
Prices for marijuana, 57
Pride in growing, 44, 57, 81, 89–93,
    95–96, 98–100, 112, 140–41
Prohibition, 62, 115

Race, 16–18, 69, 72, 99, 149
RAND Corporation, 47
Raphael, Ray, 40
Reagan, Ronald, 23, 50
Resin in marijuana, 13, 56–58, 60
Reuter, Peter, 47
Rewards of growing, 88, 156–58;
    spiritual, 88–89; social, 89–91;
    intrinsic, 91–95, 100
Romans, 13
Ruderalis. *See Cannabis ruderalis*
Rural communities, 2–3, 9, 131;
    Cash economies in, 5; Culture,
    3–6, 133, 158; Drug enforce-
    ment, 3, 149; Drugs in, 3, 146;
    Setting for growing, 3, 9, 72, 106,
    110–11, 148, 156; As tranship-
    ment points, 3
Russia, 54

Sativa. *See Cannabis sativa*
Secrecy among growers, 104–7,
    132, 152, 157

Seizure of marijuana, 1–2, 31–32,
    35, 39, 42, 48, 59, 65, 68–69, 72,
    74; *See also* Marijuana, eradica-
    tion
Self-esteem, 43–44, 128
Senior citizens: and marijuana
    growing, 40
Shawnee National Forest, 62, 142
Sheriffs, 3, 5, 43, 64, 105, 109, 129,
    131, 135–39, 142–43, 147–48,
    151
Sinsemilla, 32, 34, 54, 56–60, 68,
    74, 82–83, 97–99, 144
Smuggling drugs, 5–6, 40–41, 53,
    108; Marijuana, 48, 51
Social rewards of growing. *See*
    Rewards of growing
South America, 7, 14, 18–19, 84
Southeast Asia, 2, 7
Spiritual rewards of growing. *See*
    Rewards of growing
State police, 1, 3, 135–36, 138–39,
    148, 151
Stress from growing, 86–87
Synthetic drugs, 3, 78

Taiwan, 12
Task forces against drugs, 3, 138
Techniques of neutralization, 114
Tennessee, 8, 15, 38, 135, 148–50,
    152
Tetrahydrocannabinol. *See* THC
Texas, 2, 17, 42, 48
THC, 55, 57
Tobacco, 7, 13–14, 19, 21, 25, 83,
    112, 115–17, 132, 152, 155
Trafficking in drugs, 40
Typology of growers, 9, 41, 75–76;
    See also Hustlers; Pragmatists;
    Communal growers

Uchida, Craig, 3

Unemplyoment and growing, 62, 68, 73; *See also* Economic incentives

U.S. foreign policy, 47

U.S. Pharmacopoeia, 16

Vermont, 130

Vietnam, 18, 49–50, 111

Vietnam war, 47, 50, 71

Villa, Poncho, 14

Violence, Marijuana use and, 14, 17, 19, 23, 25; Growing and, 29, 38, 47, 101, 107–112, 132, 141–45, 150, 153, 155, 158; By the police, 108–110;

War on drugs, 2

Warner, Roger, 40, 44

Washington, George, 15

Weapons. *See* Guns

West Indies, 18

Wild marijuana 32, 34, 54, 60, 63, 65, 68, 74, 96–98, 100, 153; *See also* Hemp

Wisconsin, 2, 15

Women as growers, 71

World War II, 10, 15, 54, 68, 78, 149

World War I, 18

About the Author

RALPH A. WEISHEIT is a Professor in the Department of Justice at Illinois State University. He is the author of *Drugs, Crime, and the Criminal Justice System* (1990), *Women, Crime, and Criminal Justice* (1988), *Order Under Law* (1988), and *Juvenile Delinquency: A Justice Perspective* (1990), among other works.